THE GIFT
IN THE
WOUND

A MEMOIR AND INTERACTIVE GUIDE
FOR MORE POSITIVE LIVING.

DIÁNE MANDLE

LIFE IN PROGRESS PUBLISHING

Book Design by Gram Telen
Published by Life in Progress
ISBN: 978-1-7334042-2-8
Published 2023

This book is dedicated to Sarasvati, the Hindu Goddess of knowledge, music, art, wisdom, and learning.

CONTENTS

What Others Are Saying 9

Foreward. 11

Prologue 15

1: The Men Down Under 19

2: Granny 21

3: Life with Maman 25

4: Dad. 31

5: New Rochelle High School, 1969. 40

6: London 1972 45

7: The Workers Revolutionary Party 54

8: Aix-en-Provence. 61

9: The Freezer 68

10: Love with Blinders 71

11: Diagnosis 78

12: Zen 83

13: A Room Near the Kitchen 91

14: To Amherst 94

15: A Revelation 97

16: Sweet Murielle 101

17: The Snake Pit 106

18: Parenting Alone 109

19: Africa, 1986 116

20: India—Excerpts 127

21: Craig 134

22: Marlene 141

23: Fire! 144

24: Cuba, 1988 147

25: Ana 155

26: Salsa! Sunday Night. Ten O'clock.. 158

27: Rotary 161

28: Cancer Society 165

29: Nepal, 2000 168

30: Sound Shaman Road Trip
      (Who Says Concert Touring Is Romantic?) 179

31: Biking. 189

32: The Gift in the Wound 195

Epilogue 199

Acknowledgments 209

About the Author. 211

WHAT OTHERS ARE SAYING

Diáne Mandle revolutionizes the autobiography with her latest book, The Gift in the Wound.

Diáne engages the reader by sharing only pivotal moments from her fascinating life in vignettes. Each brief and charming chapter ends with provocative questions to invite readers to reflect on their own life experiences and to appreciate the "gifts in the wounds" in their own journeys.

Diáne has lived quite the life as the progeny of a beautiful but narcissistic French ballerina and Jewish American World War II soldier turned successful costume jewelry businessman. She becomes a Bohemian theater artist during the 1960s and 70s in Europe and the US. Later, as a single mother with two young sons to raise, Diáne takes a bold turn that results in her going from welfare to being a clever leader of respectable local civic organizations. But even though she is on her way to conventional success, she is unhappy and stifled. So, she then again makes another bold and risky change and follows her heart. This leads her on a path to become a sound and energy healer and performer who has touched thousands of lives over the last 25 years.

The Gift in the Wound is a compelling page turner! Diáne resists the temptation to go into copious details or comprehensive chronology that could have easily warranted a 300+ page memoir. (However, I do hope there will be a The Gift in the Wound, Part 2. I personally would love to read more about her magical life and work as a healer.)

The Gift in the Wound makes for an inspiring and entertaining individual read but would also be delightful to read with others in groups, classes, or book clubs.

Lil Glamben

www.menopausalsuperpowers.com

Diane Mandle's The Gift in the Wound reveals a common thread in our humanity, first, via the confessional disclosures shared and personal wisdom gleaned from her well-travelled life, and second, in the parallel stories she invites us to create as we dare to answer the soul-stirring questions she poses. Brilliant.

William Tyler

FOREWARD

O ne of the most venerable of forms in writing, autobiography can also be slippery for a reader. Is the author writing from a place of veracity? Exaggeration? Whimsy? Semi-fiction even, with an ax to grind? Sorting it out can be a bit much.

In this mosaic of vignettes from her life, Diáne Mandle springs something a bit different on us. She comes squarely from a place of altruism. Her stories conclude with a frank address to the reader; after deftly unfolding descriptions of an almost dizzying variety of experiences, Diáne asks us to reflect on specific questions our own lives offer, and that we do.

As a visual artist, I too am a practitioner of the sort of self-guided exploration that Diáne embodies - adventuring largely without a map, afloat in a sea of creative endeavor – and so her stories and the invitations to investigate my own inner space, my life rafts, are moving and useful.

Diáne has carved out of a life from a series of improbable steps and offers them up in plain view. Chance meetings on the plains of Africa, back alleys of London, lodges in the Langtang Valley, board rooms of Boston, strum the heartstrings and invite us to compare and formulate the whys and wherefores of our own existence. Diáne touches on her travels, physical and otherwise, around the world through Nepal, India, Africa, Cuba, France and America.

Easing (or falling, sometimes charging) in or out of relationships with a headstrong Flemish dancer, controversial Zen master, cancer patients, students of hers at the local penitentiary, revolutionaries, a leading Hollywood actress, her own ex-prima ballerina mother, earth-gong guru life-partner... she shares questions of her own and lessons learned. She bears two sons of Shakespearean flavor, each quite different from the other. Navigates a variety of occupations. Partners with men who also follow the beat of a different drum. Herself a nomad - restless adventurer, risk taker - Diáne eventually puts down roots.

We find this person of real-world grit landing as an international leader in one of the most starry eyed of professions - sound healer, using Tibetan bowls, gongs and other ancient instruments. Helping others, doing it through loving application and science of the cosmic music of the spheres.

The ephemeral and the concrete crash together in this book in ways surprising and pleasing at every turn. Each chapter is a separate and unique tale, yet by the end of the book we see the pattern: a life with plenty of mire.

Out of it all, many a lotus flower rises and blooms, and we along with them. Read with an open heart. You may be glad that she has tread where you have not, so that you can enjoy mystery and adventure without the bruising of shins – and soul – that goes along with a life of such searching.

Richard Hawk

May 29, 2023
Encinitas, California

PROLOGUE

The young woman in Casamance, a small village in Senegal, was squatting in the dirt next to her tiny thatched hut as I walked past her during my stay in Africa. We smiled at one another. I was probably the only white person she had ever seesn, but she motioned to me to come sit next to her. Bone thin though many months pregnant, she was preparing her midday meal and insisted we share it. The meal was a bowl of warm water with stringy pieces of white bread floating in it. I accepted her generosity of spirit amid her dire circumstances and felt deeply humbled, realizing that a situation I judged as tragic could be a moment of honor for her.

Fleeting moments of other people's lives that have intersected with mine have changed the course of my life, shifted a perception, or touched me in a way that made me pause and feel deeply. These precious, brief encounters have all contributed to my slow process of awakening.

In this, my second book, *The Gift in the Wound*, I will share with you my journey from growing up in a dysfunctional bicultural family, to my time in Europe as an actress, to my return to the US as a single mother on welfare and onward to a more stable and successful life. I will chronicle difficult relationships with men and my rise in the professional world, first as an NPR radio producer and then as a director of Chamber of Commerce and American Cancer Society chapters. I will relate stories of travels around the world. For all my meandering, these phases of my life led me to the study of energy medicine and healing with Tibetan bowls, and to the stability I now enjoy in my life.

Stability? What's that? To me it's like walking on Jell-O, trying to remain upright in a world of ever-changing chaos and adventure. It's walking through life learning to hold on to a sense of authenticity, integrity, and joy, despite feeling confusion and fear.

Each experience that led me to my present life has been a teacher. Each teacher a guide. Each guide an angel.

Imagine being exposed as a child to numerous cultures and languages each year while traveling in Europe with your French mother; think of the imprint of that. Traveling back then gifted me with a broader perspective in life than many of my peers had, and exposed me to a plethora of sounds in the form of languages and music. And the imprint held. As an adult, nothing could keep me from traveling the world, and I know that encounters with different places and cultures influenced my love of the sound healing work I do today.

Often, it has seemed that each adventure was its own unrelated story, with a different part of me showing up in each situation. But looking back I can see that all of my stories represent the Tibetan Buddhist principal of *the interrelationship of all things.* My life has the feel of a mosaic, with pieces of me all over the place, yet a thread winds its way through all. The journey continues to progress with me in it, hopefully learning to navigate life's joys and trials with aplomb, learning to be a better person as the days roll by.

If I have learned anything, it is that the walk through life is about maintaining. In this book I will share some of the pivotal experiences that have brought me to this understanding. They are not presented in chronological order. Many things happened between one story and the next, but what I share are the most memorable moments of my blip on the screen of being alive in this great universe. In retrospect I recognize that the resilience as a result of these experiences is the gift. My hope is that these stories will inspire you to reflect on the experiences in your own life that have brought special gifts—even if you did not recognize them in the moment. There are questions for you to answer at the end of each chapter. Let them be a catalyst for you to begin your own memoir.

1

THE MEN DOWN UNDER

I sit in one of the metal chairs bolted to the floor in the sparse gray waiting room at Vista Jail. *Be careful*, I warn myself. *Don't walk up to the white line on the floor yet.* I have observed the accepted routine with other visitors ahead of me in the queue. *The attendant behind the glass window will call you on her speaker when it's your turn, and then you'll make the exchange: driver's license for a visitor's pass.*

Gripped by a sense of doom, I pass through a series of thick, heavy metal doors. Click: I step through the first one, arriving in a square space between doors. Click: the second door, heavy as a refrigerator, opens; I push through into a long corridor. A few photos of past and present administrators set in cheap frames line its gray lifeless wall.

Then a staircase down. *Good God. How far underground can we get?* I nod to the people working in offices behind more glass windows protected by metal bars. *It is so creepy in here.* I take in the angry men, drunk men, tattooed and despondent men staring blankly from envelope-sized windows in the doors of holding cells.

We walk on to the elevator, the guard and I. More metal doors to open. Clank, clank. Down again and still more down into the abyss, then through another corridor past more men in single cells, whose eyes I now avoid. *Do not change the neutral expression on your face*, I advise myself. I need to appear as if this is no big deal, but my stomach is in a knot.

Finally we reach our destination. I look around. I'm in a large open space below three adjoining groups of cells, each containing thirty-two men Each quad consists of an open balcony floor lined with cells that are furnished with two bunk beds and a toilet. Before me, men are seated in the cafeteria under florescent lights. There are tables, plastic chairs, one small, rolling bookcase. A large television hangs on the wall, blasting. The felons look at me skeptically as I stand before them with my Tibetan bowls, all slight five-feet-two of me, hoping to impart something worthwhile. *Can I do this?* I ask myself. This is a story I will return to.

2

GRANNY

She was the love of my life, seemingly ageless, and the absolute best, most fun person to be around. I loved her plumpness, her kindness, her softly wrinkled jowls, her energy, and her stories. I loved that she maintained a free spirit and did not fit the traditional mold of a grandmother.

"Oh my God, Granny, you really risked your life during the war smuggling food from Valberg to give to your Jewish friends hiding from the Nazis? You hid live chickens under your coat on the bus? The SS could have stopped you so easily! You were so courageous—but you must have been terrified."

She shrugs as if it was nothing and begins playing her electric piano. Soon she is singing "Alexander's Ragtime

Band" with the sophisticated accent of a French woman schooled in England.

Summer mornings I open the shutters in Valberg to the glorious vision of the sun bathing the fathomless gorge below, and I smile. I know that this time here with my darling Granny is worth every penny of the babysitting money I saved all year in the States. This picturesque ski station in the French Alps is where I spend the happiest moments of my life.

Granny plunks down raucous Elvis songs on her electric piano. She serves homemade tarts and hot chocolate as our Sunday evening meal. *Woohoo!* this is *my* grandmother, constantly adventuring, finding ways to be generous, and leaving her mark on me.

"Diáne, we go to gather mushrooms and wild strawberries to bring to my old friend Florence. It eeze a long walk through ze mountains, but she has nothing but her rabbits, and she will be happy for some company and our leetle gifts."

Granny inspired my passion for travel by spinning stories of beautiful African women she met during the ten years she lived in Madagascar with her son, who worked as a doctor there. *Women swayed so gracefully in zair colorful dresses as zay walked weeth huge bas-kets filled with mangos or bananas on zair heads. Always children were running beside zem laughing and playing. People 'ad so little but zay 'ad lives filled weethe love and community.*

Witnessing the generosity of a people who had so little taught her to find something positive in every situation. Years later, when her eyes betrayed her and she went blind, the dancing shadows before her became the characters in her stories. She always found a way to be creative.

"Ma petite Diáne, can you write a story for me? Phillip and Marie are preparing for a secret adventure in space. Every night zay disappear under their bed sheets and climb into zair spaceship des-tined for za moon. If Papa or Maman come into ze room, zay pretend to be sleeping and begin to whisper again only when ze bedroom door is clos-ed ..."

When my aunt could no longer care for her, my aging Granny was moved to a small room in a private hillside home just above Nice where she was cared for by a mature couple until the age of 101. On my way back to the States from a vacation, I stop to visit, knowing this will be the last time I see her. Although frail, she always finds a way to be generous and gently presses a few francs into my palm. *Achète-toi quelque chose de spéciale, ma chérie.* (Buy something special for yourself, my sweetheart).

Leaving her is excruciating. My heart aches with the knowledge that I will never be in her presence again.

How does one suspend a moment into forever? The touch of my lips on her ever-soft face, the honey earthy scent of her skin, the crackly sound of her voice. These things I long to take with me as I kiss her—our last kiss. As I walk out the door and turn to get a final glimpse, she is sitting at her kitchen table, knife in hand, feeling around for a piece of bread to slice for herself.

When someone dies, someone you have loved deeply, I think part of her stays inside you: her voice, the feeling of her, and the impression she has left on your life. Any amount of creativity or courage I have is a direct offspring of my grandmother's spirit—her gift to me. I just hope she knew how much I loved her, and that I love her still.

Granny

Questions:

- Who was the biggest positive influence in your life.
- What did you learn from this person?
- Is there something you do or can do to act upon what you have learned?
- How do you carry their memory forward?

3

LIFE WITH MAMAN

"Well, maybee eet his not een my naatoure to lee-zen!"

The words delivered in her thick French accent smack of the dismissive tone of the bourgeoisie when addressing those of lesser standing. But the sting is worse—it is my mother speaking to me.

Still svelte and stunningly handsome, a former prima ballerina with the Opéra de Paris and a war bride, my mother never abandoned her aristocratic roots. It was always "The world according to Charlotte." A world whose job it was to revolve around her, fulfilling the unvoiced but always alluded-to expectations I would come to understand through the shaming that occurred if I missed the mark.

"Oh I 'ad a gol-den childhoud in our Rue de France villa in Nice. We played on ze marble staircases and threw littol tings at ze crystal chandeliers. We 'ad a merveilleuse nanny, a cook, servants—many goud tings. I never 'ad to remember where my ballet rehearsals wer, le chauffeur knew and ee took me zere."

In America Maman had expectations and a disillusioned image of the land of plenty: no outside help, and a gaggle of kids.

"But, Mom, for once I really want you to listen to me, to hear me. Please."

But this is futile because my beautiful, photogenic mother could be the poster child for the classic narcissist. It always has to be about her—unless "it" is something unpleasant, and then it can *never* be *because* of her.

"Every theeng I doo eez out of obligation."

Does she have a clue what words like that might mean to me, her child? With each small insult, part of me retreats into a place where my battered spirit floats in nothingness, not even in pain. Outwardly she appears a martyr, the charming French immigrant courageously fulfilling her family obligations—which we are never allowed to forget.

"Mon Dieu, mon Dieu, mais qu'est-ce que j'ai fait pour avoir des enfants comme ça?" (My God, my God, but what did I do to deserve children like this?)

It isn't exactly a compliment, chanted as she slumps over, head in hands. Her words, repeated like the chorus of a tragic country and western ballad, chip away at the fragile protective membrane of my spirit.

It is confusing to be her child. Sometimes, as a special treat, Maman takes me by train into the city to see the Joffrey or a Balanchine ballet at Lincoln Center, then out to the Russian Tea Room for cakes. I, dressed in my red velvet dress with a satin border and patent leather shoes, feeling like the luckiest girl in the world. On those days she is fun to be with because we are sharing something so dear to us, and a happy banter goes on between us about who was the best dancer or which costume we liked the most. But it will change in a heartbeat if I keep her waiting a moment too long by pausing to look in a shop window. *"Tu me donnes mal au jambes. J'ai des varices à cause de toi. Je ne peu pas rester debout comme ça à t'attendre."* (You are hurting my legs. You are giving me varicose veins. I cannot stand here like this waiting for you.)

Years later when I have children of my own, we are often invited over for a meal, and then subjected to a harangue about how tiring it is for her to cook for us. At other times, my mother is a cheerleader for me—until she isn't. She appears and disappears depending on whether my situation reflects well on her or not. I cannot depend on her for emotional support unless it is of use to her.

Right out of the womb, dance is my passion and Maman sees that. The record player blasts *Carmen, Aida, Swan Lake* while she does a pas de deux through the living room with a broom as her partner. As it does for her, dance feels like a lifeline to me. So, as a mere toddler, I am enrolled at the Mimi Kellerman School of Dance, the custom for a blossoming ballerina.

We rehearse steps at home together in preparation for my role in my first recital at age three. I am following in her footsteps, creating profound ties between us. I sense her pride and feel full of being loved. We share in the joys of the music, steps, and costumes. But suddenly, I am suffering from stomachaches and passing blood. It is a polyp in my colon, at the age of four. I am forced to drink disgusting barium for months with both my mother and the doctor insisting it is really a strawberry milkshake. Children are not stupid.

"I don't like this drink. It's not stawburry. It's not, Maman."

"Mais oui, Diáne. It eez *straberry. You must drink it maintenant!!"*

The night before the operation, I circle the dinner table, forbidden to eat while my siblings sit before their plates triumphantly. My bottom lip quivers as I am repeatedly pushed away from the table. No one explains that I must fast before the operation, or what is going to happen in the hospital the next day.

A group of strangers accompany the rolling table I am on. They keep telling me to blow up the balloons as a mask is being pushed into my face. *Where are the balloons? There are no balloons! They are trying to kill me!* Screaming, I fight with all my four-year-old might until several nurses hold me down and the ether does its job.

My ten days in the hospital leave Maman worried that the scar from the surgery will open if I exert myself. Ballet is deemed dangerous, so my dream of being a ballerina, along with half my colon, are whooshed away at the tender age of four. A little piece of my soul smashed—but not broken.

· · ·

"*I ham pu-tting gold bricks in zaair heads,*" says Maman defiantly, addressing Monseigneur at St. Pius X Church in New Rochelle, New York. It is May and she has come to pull us out of our Catholic school for our annual visit to France. He wants us to stay the term but she always gets her way. It drives the teachers crazy for us to be pulled out of school early and brought back late. But away we go—to Nice, Paris, Italy, Switzerland for months at a time.

"*Tant pis*" (too bad). Those are the *best* months of our lives. Maman is happy then, surrounded by her "real" family: her brother and sister, my amazing grandmother, and all the nieces, nephews, and cousins. She gets all the attention she needs and we kids are absorbed in the bosom of familial love.

"*Les enfants, get your bas-ketts. We will collect champignons and fraises for le picnik. Your cousins ave brot salami, fromages, baguettes, tartes au pommes, and chocolate. Zen we can go to le petit festival for a dance and a glass of wine.*"

I am satiated by love and care in France. Dad stays in New York to work, occasionally flying over to join us for a week or so. A Jewish businessman, he busts his butt to provide for us kids and his ever-demanding French Catholic ballerina wife. At home, my parents argue. But for those few months in France, we don't have to hear them fighting. Or feel the crushing abandonment when Maman runs from the room instead of protecting us as he rages.

In France, we don't have to be afraid.

Maman

Questions:

- Please describe your relationship with your mother.
- What is your best and worst memory?
- How did your biggest challenge with your mother resolve?
- What could have been better?
- What positive take-away do you recognize from it from where you stand now?

4

DAD

"Fairytale wedding: French Catholic, stunningly beautiful, prima ballerina swept away by the handsome lieutenant who liberated her country during WW II settle in New Rochelle, NY."

That's how the newspaper described it. After the honeymoon camping trip across the US, Dad worked as the president of his costume jewelry business, building quite a name for himself, while Maman had five babies. All five would witness the storybook marriage turning into a lifetime of miscommunication, dysfunction, and sadness.

Despite the traumas of our childhood, I know Dad did his best. He had his own hell to contend with when we were young, scrambling to provide for a growing family and his dissatisfied spouse. And the war raged on inside him, fueling his wrath. He loved us—he really did—but the scars of battle had burned deep. Much of the time, he felt like a time bomb waiting to go off. But he couldn't help how he was.

· · ·

Most of the time, being his little girl isn't much fun. Often, it is scary. Each night when he comes home from work, the house develops a kind of chill.

"Daddy will be home in a minute. Better make sure the place is completely cleaned up. No stray toys around, or else."

We must line up at the door to kiss him hello, hoping he is in a good mood. Otherwise … Otherwise he walks around the house rubbing his thumb and third finger together. It is an unconscious twitch that means trouble. Before the night is over, one of us will feel the brunt of the fury he has contained during his workday. It may erupt in words. Or in a slap to the face. Or as an order to go to bed without dinner. The infraction that triggers it doesn't need to be big—almost anything will do when he's looking for a way to vent.

There is a place inside myself where I go to hide when things get too frightening, an unreachable, untouchable place in the ethers where I feel safe. It will take much of my adult life to realize that when friction arises in any relationship, I retreat into avoidance. And that there is no real safety in that.

• • •

During the summers when we do not go to France with my mother, Dad rents a rustic wooden cabin near a lake in Great Barrington, Massachusetts, for a couple of weeks. There are community dinners where we get to see our friends from other summer visits: big campfires, grilled corn, hot dogs, s'mores, and singalongs. Such fun. Dad is always charming on those occasions.

Mr. Victor is an older man who gives dance lessons down at the lodge. Each morning I scamper down there and he stops his class so I can come in and give him a little kiss.

"*Oh, thank you, little sweetheart. Now my day is perfect, just like you.*"

He makes me feel so good that I decide to adopt Mr. Victor.

"*Would you be my daddy?*"

"*Why, honey? You have a perfectly good daddy.*"

"*But my daddy gets mad all the time and you are fun.*"

Mr. Victor declines the invitation. But he also helps me see all the ways my own daddy loves me, and he assures me that he will always be my special friend. Years later, when I am eleven, my mother will tell me that Mr. Victor was a "gay queen" who died of AIDS. I will be deeply saddened to lose my warm and attentive friend, around whom I always felt valued.

Dad isn't *always* in a bad mood. When he's in a good mood, he calls me "Poupoutte" and bounces me up and down on his knees. My daddy is tall, with warm brown eyes and a balding head. Sometimes we go to his office in the city, just the two of us, on the train. I get the window seat and watch the world rush by while he reads the paper like all the other fathers do. My favorite part is coming into the looooonnnnggg, dark tunnel to Grand Central. When we exit the train car my daddy holds my hand so I don't get lost in the crowd and we walk a few blocks to the Fifth Avenue building where he *always* says to the elevator man:

"*Jake, you remember my mother, don't you?*"

I hang around the showroom of Robert Mandle, Inc., pulling out trays of his fine fashion costume jewelry to admire. There are glass jars of hard candies, and I am allowed to have a few pieces of butterscotch. His staff calls him "Mr. Mandle" and exclaims, "*What a cutie!*"—about me! At the end of the day I always get a little pin I like that he has designed.

· · ·

Standing up to Dad earns his respect and the privilege of shared intimacies that none of my siblings experience. I am only about ten when he tells me about the time in the war when he squatted next to his friend who was holding his brains in his hands, and Dad could do nothing but watch him die. He felt useless, and heartbroken, traumatized. He tells me about all the starving kids who fought to get a stick of chewing gum from the GIs—sometimes the only food they had. Our complaining when we don't like something that was served for dinner drives him crazy.

"You will eat what you are given, or you will have it cold in the morning."

He mellowed considerably in his old age, and his angry spurts became more pathetic than frightening. He grew older, slower, and nicer—much nicer. He loved to show us off to his friends. He supported my dreams the best he could by telling me that I could have whatever I wanted if I raised half the money for it. He would chip in the other half. Dad came to opening night of every one of my theatrical performances and even traveled to England to do that. I felt so loved when he showed up and took me and my friends out to dinner after a show. He tried very hard to be a good man. He was a good man.

. . .

I am seven and our family is at Daddy's friend Chick's house for a picnic. I am in the kitchen being a little helper by holding a tray with glasses of Coca-Cola destined for the party in the yard. Chick kneels in front of me, patting me on the head with one hand: *"You're such a good little girl."* The other hand is in my panties, exploring parts of me he has no right to.

When it is over I go downstairs, feeling invisible among the laughing and joking people. I want to die. Part of me does die on that day. But nobody notices. I want to be rescued, but even my daddy doesn't see me then. Inside is my little voice saying, *Help me.* No one does.

When as an adult with children of my own, I gave this poem to my father he said that when he read it, he cried all night, asked for my forgiveness and said that if he had known, he would have killed the guy. Finally, a place for healing to begin.

Letter to a Boyfriend

I ask for help.
So many reasons not to.
A continuum you do not comprehend
A progression of ghosts
Precede the asking.
Formulating words,
Negotiating phantoms.
Finally, the deed is done
I stand paralyzed
Anticipating response.

I ask for your help.
I can now because I am all grown up
Or so it seems.
Really, I am seven years old again
Standing in the kitchen of my father's friend's home
Holding the tray with sodas.
What a good girl to help at this friendly picnic.
His hands are in my pants
He is feeling me and pushing his fingers up inside me
My mouth cannot speak

It tries to cry out
Cry for help but no words come
I want to die.

When he is finished he pats me on the behind
And sends me out to serve the Coca-Colas.
No one notices that I am breaking apart
I want to die
No one notices anything at all
I am invisible and no one is helping me.

Later, much, years
When words come
I ask for help
My father disbelieves me.
I am making this up,
I should be ashamed of myself.

I am. I am ashamed
I am invisible and nobody comes to help
I want to die.

In the moment between when I ask
And when you respond
I am seven years old again

Help me and the ending changes
Blow me off and I am invisible again,
Quietly wanting to die.

I keep choosing men who say no to me
Men who don't care what the ending is
Men like my molester
He didn't care and you don't care

I keep trying to make you care
Trying to change the ending.

Years later, Dad puts my hand on his heart that I can feel breaking as he stifles tears, his face contorted with emotion. *I love you so much* he squeaks out through gritted teeth in his final moments in the hospital. It is the first time he has ever said those words to me. They are like a balm to my soul that I have needed to hear for a lifetime. There have been plenty of "luv ya's" but never such a full-fledged declaration, and his words open another door to the healing of my own wounds.

I love him so much too.

Dad

Questions:

- Describe your father.
- What was your relationship with your father like?
- What is your best and worst memory?
- How did your biggest challenge with your father resolve?
- What could have been better?
- What positive take-away do you recognize from it from where you stand now?

5

NEW ROCHELLE HIGH SCHOOL, 1969

Oh my God! My high school is burning up!

The beautiful gothic-style buildings tucked beside idyllic twin lakes are being devoured by flames. It is horrific, this act of arson. Nothing is spared: the science labs, the library, everything we left in our lockers—all will vanish in the fire.

Just a few days later, we take our final exams at the junior high school where they have made room for us. Still in shock, we rise at dawn for double sessions there and sit for the tests, bleary eyed.

I will not return to this time or place. I have survived my senior year, and now I'm looking forward to spending a summer hitchhiking through Europe with my best friend, Laura. A grand way to just *forgetaboutit*. It's time for fun.

I really like Laura. She trusts me completely, almost blindly, an especially valued trait when I am not quite sure what I am doing- which will be the case on several occasions during our trip. Laura is a shy, slim girl with a long neck, short boyish hair and huge eyes. She often seems uncertain but I am usually very certain so we complement each other. What I love the most about Laura is her voice. She sings like an angel and will do so with very little prodding. It is the only really un-shy thing about her and a very good thing when traveling as a way to meet people. Laura's father is a big man who seems to derive pleasure in disempowering his daughter. Some people put others down to make themselves feel better. Maman does this too sometimes. He is mean and she survives with her great sense of humor and her songs. But something inside her seems like a kicked puppy. A trip to Europe together is just the thing to help her see herself in a better light- away from his eyes. And I thrive upon the admiration and trust I am receiving from my friend because I feel purposeful ,valued and seen by her.

We have a pitiful amount of money between us so rely on our ability to pick up cute guys and get them to buy us dinner. This ploy usually ends up with one of us feigning a belly- ache and needing to get back to our room quickly. But the fellows in Avignon were skeptical and followed us back to what we thought was a BnB to make sure we had to stay in all night. They parked outside and waited.

Laura, being a quick study noticed me kissing all my friends and relatives upon meeting. So when a guy walked into the hallway outside our room she immediately said 'Bonjour' and kissed him on both cheeks. This is when I knew we were not in a BnB. The guy grabbed her as I fiddled with the room key in the lock. Just in time I pulled her into the room and locked the door behind us as the man yelled unsavory words at us. An hour later we were in the bedroom of a big house in the country just outside Avignon. Here, I am not quivering with fear. Thelioness within me reared it's head and my theatrical skills are put to the test:

"I'm gonna tell you something, Laura, but don't freak out. Nothing's gonna happen. I know how to handle things. I know you don't understand French, so you have to be ready to act fast if I tell you to do something.

The guys who were parked outside the brothel brought us here from the brothel after we figured out it wasn't a B&B, jumped out the window and went down the fire escape. They laughed at us and told us they would take us to a safe place for the night.

"You know this is their friend's house, right? It was nice of them to get us out of there, but now they think we owe them a favor—I just heard them talking through the wall. They're gonna bust in here any minute. Just let me handle it, and stay calm. Okay? Okay? Never mind what they say; you just have to trust me. I don't have time to transla—

"*Quoi alors? Qu'est-ce que c'est* ça? *Allez mettre les pantalons! Vous êtes débile d'entrer comme ça. Sans pantalon. Ce n'est pas convenable. C'est grossier.*"

(What? What is this? Go put some pants on. You are ridiculous coming in like that. Without pants. It isn't appropriate. And it's rude.)

"*Si vouz avez quelque chose à dire, allez mettre les pantalons et après vous pourrez revenir et nous parlerons. Allez, vous connards.*"

(If you have something to say, go put your pants on, and then you can come back and we will talk. Now go, you assholes.)

They turn and walk out sheepishly. Laura has turned a pale shad of green. Understandable, with these stupid guys coming in trying to test their luck with us. I am sure they are going to powwow out there and come back again, acting all brazen, trying to preserve their egos. They are just as young and stupid as we are.

"*Laura, grab your bag and jump out the window with me before they come back. We'll pick a few apples on the way through the orchard so we have something to eat till we get somewhere. We have to run now. We can hitchhike once we get to the road.*"

Laura doesn't hesitate. She springs up at the ready to follow me anywhere. And so begin the raucous adventures of two girls let loose in Europe during the summer of 1969 hitchhiking around, picking up boys, hanging out on topless beaches. Living on the edge in a manner that still defines so much of my life, in ways both pleasurable and painful learning about the importance of discernment.

Questions:

- What is the most risky thing you have done in your life?
- Why did you do it?
- How did you feel while doing it?
- Describe how you resolved the situation.
- What are your thoughts and feelings about it now?

6

LONDON 1972

"It's not that she wouldn't. It's not that she couldn't, but she's the loneliest girl on the block."

This said at Old Bailey in a noble British accent delivered by an ancient magistrate in formal robes, complete with a white wig.

My friend Anna pokes me and whispers out of the side of her mouth, *"This is serious—don't you dare giggle or you'll be thrown in jail."*

The magistrate clears the courtroom. Then he asks me, *"Young lady, do you know what an erection is?"*

"Yes, Your Honor."

"*And do you mean to tell me that your young man never had one with you?*"

"*He did, Your Honor, but at the point of intimacy he realized that he was not inclined to go further with me. He discovered that he was not that way inclined.*"

Moment of silence.

"*Well, for God's sake. Give the girl a divorce.*"

And that is the end of my life as Mrs. Peter Ramsey Nicholson, which had begun several months prior in another courtroom.

• • •

It is a simple ceremony. Peter arrives with a bunch of withered dandelions, guitar in hand, singing, "*A shepherd's life is a lonely life, ain't got a girl, don't have a wife. That's why you'll find me fucking she-e-e-ep.*"

Some of the cast of Liquid Theater serve as witnesses. We're a motley bunch dressed in costumes acquired from local theatrical thrift shops: feather boas; top hats; long, floating gowns; a red velvet king's robe. We have all dropped acid to celebrate both the wedding and the final performance of Liquid Theater that would occur in the evening after six months of working together under the arches of Charing Cross.

Peter is a long-haired blond with a space between his front teeth and an easy manner- kind of like a young, blond Donovan type. When the Home Office announces my impending deportation for working in London without the proper visa, he steps forward to marry me. His girlfriend doesn't mind, and the months we spend writing bogus love letters to one another, pretending to be a proper couple, are fun. As soon as my passport arrives, the marriage is annulled on the grounds of non-consummation.

Liquid Theater is a London phenomenon of the early '70s, lovingly referred to as "the touchy feely show." We have built the performance area ourselves, the London cast of an American-run show that also has a troupe in Paris. We perform two shows nightly, leading folks through a maze of experiential activities, some while blindfolded, and all leading to an explosive group dance with a live rock band. By the end of the show, even the most conservative participants are half naked.

I am in London studying theater for my junior year abroad and enjoying elocution lessons so I can sound like a Brit. When the auditions come along I am thrilled to be cast so it's all over for college. For the next four and a half years, I perform as Baby Bear in holiday pantomimes, as the epileptic sister in *The Effect of Gamma Rays on Man in the Moon Marigolds*, in endless lunchtime theater shows, and in the Red Buddha Theater, run by Japanese virtuoso percussionist Stomu Yamash'ta.

"If I could ever be in a show like this, it would satisfy my every theatrical yearning," I exclaim after seeing a Red Buddha performance. Six days later it becomes my reality.

• • •

My nose is only slightly fractured; just enough to leave a small bump and blood everywhere, but the hospital insists on keeping me overnight.

"*Stomu, I do not know how to do a back flip off my partner's shoulders. And there is no padding on the cement floor if I fall,*" I say at the rehearsal.

"*You don't fall,*" he replies. Very Japanese of him. All it takes is 100 percent concentration, absolute confidence, and the image in my head of doing a back flip.

I do not fall. But the heels of the guy in front of me hit me in the nose as *he* does a back flip, and I pass out, gushing blood. They drag me to the corner of the room to recover.

"*You have to take her to the hospital! You cannot just leave her there bleeding and unconscious,*" shouts the only other Westerner in the room.

This is a problem. The Red Buddha Theatre troupe is leaving for its five-week tour of Italy in the morning and I need to be with them. I am one of only a couple of non-Japanese women in the troupe of forty-five, and I represent the women when negotiating issues that come up during the tour. So I let myself out of the hospital, battered nose and all, because there is no way I will not be leaving with them in the morning.

Stomu Yamash'ta is the prolific Japanese percussionist who conceived and directs the Red Buddha Theater. In his own amazing performances, he has drums, gongs, chimes, and all varieties of things to strike, bang, and ting on the stage. He'll play something on one end of the stage and then suddenly, like a shape shifter, he's on the other end creating complementary rhythms. As a director he is strict, demands total focus, and creates dramatic, passionate scenes from great simplicity.

"*What do you do?*" he asks me at the audition.

"*I am an actress.*"

"*Then act,*" he says.

Okay then. Well, as unusual as it is, I manage to improvise a wacked scene of being catapulted through the birth canal into the world. It is an untraditional audition, to say the least, but Stomu likes my creativity and hires me on the spot.

Several weeks prior, my Singaporean friend, Siva, had gifted me with tickets to a Red Buddha Theater performance at the Roundhouse, a popular London theater near Hampstead Heath known for offbeat performances. It was a heart-pumping experience. The live music, colorful costumes, mimes, masks, acrobats, and mélange of traditional Noh and avant-garde styles. I was blown away! When a couple of weeks later Siva called me to say, "*They are having auditions. Go,*" I did.

The first rehearsal is amazing. Stomu instructs me in his broken English:

"*Walk to other end of room and turn. Like to say goodbye to friends.*"

The moment I turn, arm raised in the goodbye gesture, he shouts "Freeze! *Now melt to floor. Berry slow. Like melting.*" I do.

Other cast members are given similar directions. Man with a bike, woman with children, boy pushing a vegetable cart . . . All kinds of the most normal early morning activities end with a massive *freeze!* and a slow-motion melting to the ground, all to the sound of a single eerie, high-pitched note on violin. This is Hiroshima the moment the bomb dropped. Massive death amid the most ordinary daily life. The scene is so simple, so powerful. This is Yamash'ta's style.

Rehearsals are rigorous. *"Aww, Stomu, can't we rest? We just traveled eight hours on the train to get here."*

"No, we work now. All costumes and full energy. Must be best for show tomorrow."

Exhausting, exhilarating, life changing. Working in a Japanese company teaches me to raise the bar in my own acting career forever. There is no room for whining; the group is more important than the individual.

Our show tours all over Italy during a time when there is great political unrest. Armed soldiers encircle the theaters and the two-thousand-seat stadiums we perform in. Italians are passionate theatergoers and express their love profusely, frequently following us from one performance to another and storming the stage after the finale to shower us with kisses, flowers . . . and pieces of hashish placed in our hands as they are shaking them. We are left with the illicit drugs, terrified of being caught by the soldiers and dogs sent there to protect us.

Tonight is the dress rehearsal for our first performance in Rome, where the male lead performer, wearing a Japanese peasant robe over black tights, is doing a traditional dance with a scythe. Some of us are seated in the audience watching until our scene comes up. Suddenly he stops, walks to the front of the stage, bows, and leaves. *Unusual. A scene never stops in the middle like that.*

There is a commotion backstage. *"Erybody listen!"* Stomu shouts. *"We rearrange entire show before performance tonight."* Four hours of scrambling allow the show to go on without the lead performer. *But why?*

He is in the hospital, having slit open his leg across the hamstring and Achilles tendon during rehearsal. He will never dance again, and may not be able to walk unassisted—bad news for a mime. This we find out the next morning on our way out of town for five weeks of touring. Stomu leaves this man, who speaks neither English nor Italian, in the hospital to fend for himself because *"He not concentrated enough. Accident he own fault."*

This is the Japanese way. Just like my busted nose. Our colleague will be abandoned at an Italian hospital without a translator.

Five weeks later, on our return trip back to London, we encounter him again. But he will not be returning with us because, from his hospital bed and without the language skills of the country, he has managed to hire a violinist and book weeks of performances as a one-man show, portraying an old cripple.

Japanese people have a different mind-set about work than Westerners do. It's all about focus and resilience, with exceptionally high standards. Tired? Too bad. Sick? Work anyway. Accident? Your own fault.

During the trip home I ponder how it is that one person can forge ahead despite adversity while another just crumbles. "No obstacles, no excuses" is the winner's mind-set that has been clearly demonstrated to me.

I wonder if I have the strength of character to live my life that way.

Diane and Peter Wedding with Liquid Theater cast
Red Buddha Theatre

Questions

- What is one accomplishment you are most proud of? Why?
- What did it take for you to achieve that?.
- Did you have to give something up to do that?
- How did that feel?

7

THE WORKERS REVOLUTIONARY PARTY

In early 1970s London, a strange force of politics seemed to encompass the otherwise astute minds of my British friends. It was as if they were being swallowed up by some fast-moving virus that affected their minds, like in Ionesco's *Rhinoceros*.

This was all understandable, of course: big names and lots of promises and rhetoric were spewing forth from the Socialist Labor League (SLL), soon to become the Workers Revolutionary Party (WRP). I was a struggling actress, and the actors' equity of the Trotsky-leaning WRP movement was being guided by Corin and Vanessa Redgrave, bright stars in the worlds of theater and movies. Many of the actors and artists of that time, such as Malcolm Tierney and Glenda Jackson, were among those who gravitated to the revolutionary movement. The WRP theater company produced and toured with plays about political prisoners from Ireland, the horrors that went on in factories, the oppressed and the underdogs.

It was an opportunity to get involved with some purposeful theater and to work as a peer alongside stars of stage and screen. We gathered excitedly at the Oval House Theater in south London to rehearse our first play, about Lenin. In the unfinished basement of the theater, about twenty of us began learning the first steps of a spoof Busby Berkeley tap routine. Some of us were definitely not dancers! What fun it was to watch the stars struggle through learning the steps, mess up their lines, forget their blocking, and swear at themselves for going dry.

A new reality was awakening for me: the thought that these luminaries with their on-screen personas were actually very much like me. Here, all of us were bumbling around at the beginning of something new. My previous perceptions had deprived them of their humanness, and I had put myself down by being in awe of their image.

Just before our first performance at a huge theater in central London, Vanessa, my friend Anna, and I were sharing a dressing room. Redgrave was talking to someone through the open door to the hallway. She was complaining that she didn't know where her career was going—some sort of insecurity about having to compete with Glenda Jackson and Jane Fonda for roles. It was hard to believe my ears, so

I said, "How can you be worried? You've already made it."
She laughed and explained that your problems correspond
to whatever level you have reached in life. If you're at the
bottom of the ladder, you're competing as an actress with
others who are starting out. When you get to the top, there
are others right there next to you and fewer roles of quality
to compete for. It was all relative to where you were.

I recognized that we were all different in the level of our
struggles, but the dynamics and obstacles we had to resolve
were similar. Our insecurities, fears, joys, and sorrows as
human beings could bind us together if we just saw things
that way.

I recall hiding in the living room bookshelves as a small
girl of six, watching my parents argue. Dad was yelling,
out of control, pointing his finger at my mother, who was
frightened and sobbing. As their struggle continued, I
realized that these people whom I trusted and had placed
on a pedestal were just like me, only older. They couldn't
handle their own lives, so how could I feel secure putting
mine in their hands for safekeeping? The shock of this
discovery made me gasp—it was terrifying. If they couldn't
take care of me, who could? Oh, they would surely provide
some physical necessities—food, shelter, clothing—but
what about me, the child inside? Who would soothe my
emotions, embrace my small sorrows and joys? Who would
have the good judgment to hear my frustrations and help
me grow? At age six, I already knew it would not be my
parents. It was crushing to see these harsh realities of life,
and I didn't have the tools to know where to turn.

I had just lost my faith in people, and it would be many years before I could begin to exhale that gasp. But the experience did teach me that on some level we are all the same, regardless of race, age, or culture—and that for the most part, we all feel lost.

This knowledge was often submerged under the desire to believe in the strength and goodness of humanity. Belief in the images we put out into the world. So going into theater was a natural progression for me: a field of make-believe.

In due time, the play was ready for public performance in a large West End theater. Hundreds of factory workers and union organizers packed the place with great enthusiasm for their rights, chants of slogans, and grand declarations of actions they would take for the cause of the oppressed. As time went on, demands increased for actors to participate in the activities of the WRP: selling literature in the street, lobbying fearlessly at our places of work, attending political meetings. My actor friends were excited about the promise of better wages, agitating for contractual changes, and talking up politics at rehearsals of other theatrical productions. Everyone was getting revved up for revolution.

Anyone who questioned the radical and aggressive tactics of the WRP was ostracized verbally—including me. During the course of our second production at the Little Theater Club in the West End, the actors had frequent political meetings. I was in this community for the theater and subject matter; political party affiliation was not for me. My own friends started turning on me for refusing to join the party. Anna, my flatmate and a friend who had been like a sister to me, stopped speaking to me, angry about my so-called lack of commitment to the party. The fact that I had unresolved questions about the WRP and saw hypocrisy there was of no consequence. I couldn't disregard what I was seeing—a group of weak people binding together behind a political agenda—nor could I question anything I saw. Attempts at personal conversations were met with rhetoric and political quotations. I was being asked to accede my life to a front, an image, and I could not. As with my parents, I could see both the front and the reality.

Party members began to appear at my flat at midnight, demanding to know my whereabouts and if I was working in a non-union show. If I wasn't part of the solution, they told me, I was part of the problem. I was six years old again and there was no foreseeable solution—again. I was in a painful limbo.

My final involvement with WRP was at a meeting I attended out of curiosity, an effort to understand my own conflicts about the situation. Someone in the audience questioned the party as I had, and I sprang to that person's defense. Suddenly a man reached out and slapped me across the face.

"You're a fascist!" he said. "I'd like to kill people like you."

I was stunned, but not into silence. "A fascist," I replied, "is someone who needs to kill someone else because of a difference of opinion," and I left.

It was a typical London evening, damp and drizzling. As I walked toward the tube station, a car beeped at me. It was the person who had slapped me moments before—Malcolm Tierney was offering me a ride home.

"Is this a joke? You just hit me. What do you want to give me a ride for?"

Malcolm stepped out of the car. "Diane," he replied, "you are really such a nice person and I like you as a person." He put his arm around me. "In the meeting, that's my politics, but you are really sweet and I like you."

I drew away from him abruptly. "You're nuts. You're all a bunch of lunatics. I want nothing to do with your damned party, but if I did I'd sure as hell have the guts to live out my politics in my personal life."

Years later, after moving to Paris, I watched as my London friends left the WRP one by one, burned out and disillusioned. They laughed it off as if it was a joke they had been sucked into, and they tried to portray themselves as never really having been all that involved.

Yet our friendships remain because, in the end, love endures.

To this day that experience in London has tainted my participation in any group. I see how much the same we all are. People join together in sometimes ridiculous ways just to feel a sense of belonging, of sameness. By the same token, differences scare and threaten us. The foundation of so many social ills, especially racism, lies here. Much of my life has been spent trying to untangle the fallacies I was nurtured on, to reach an inner maturity where truth is truth and differences are just differences … nothing more, nothing less.

Questions:

- What groups do you belong to?
- What do you get from being part of these groups?
- How does your participation help you engage with others who are different from you?
- How does it create more separation from others?

8

AIX-EN-PROVENCE

"*What the hell is that sound?*" I say aloud a nanosecond before the cork explodes, spattering the thick cherry mixture all over the ceiling and walls. "*Oh fuck. Fuck shit fuck. I can't believe this.*"

I stand dumbfounded in the center of my kitchen, newly painted white. Its walls now drip with homemade cherry syrup. The recipe called for white sugar, but I, in my infinite wisdom, used brown because it seemed healthier. And now it *is* much healthier since we can't ingest it at all unless we lick it off the walls, ceiling, and floor. *Now* I understand fermentation.

Sven has just arrived from Amsterdam in an old VW van filled with three other guys just out of heroin rehab. I offer them a cold beverage of sparkling water and the remains of cherry syrup made from our own fruit tree. Somehow they have decided it would be a good idea to drive down to my house just outside Aix-en-Provence to live for a while.

Lisa and Eric share the house with me in Célony, a tiny, nondescript village consisting of a couple of dirt roads and a handful of houses just a few miles outside of Aix. Ours is a typical Provençal-style stone house amid vineyards. Red tile roof, blue-trimmed window shutters, a fig and a cherry tree in the yard.

Being a bunch of starving artists, we are determined to milk those trees for all they are worth, so we consume fig and cherry cakes, compote, preserves, and godforsaken syrup for weeks.

I had met Lisa years prior when she was in the Parisian cast of Liquid Theater. We became lifelong friends and now she has joined Eric and me in the countryside for a few months to create a two-woman show. Lisa is an olive skinned die-hard romantic with a mass of dark hair and huge brown eyes. She loves Brecht, Tolstoy, and Chekhov-all the classics. She has a determined flakiness about her that is compelling for theater.

"Oh I ham just going to ave a petit coffee wiz my cigarette because I am so fatiguée from aving lived in Paris the last ten years."

She is the type to go to the market but forget her wallet, or show up at the airport without her passport. But her sensitivity to others goes deep and her heart is large so we tolerate one another's character flaws and love each other like sisters. So it works.

Eric is my Jewish Cockney boyfriend. We met in a London pub where he sketched designs for cheap polyester dresses to be produced in east London sweatshops. To a recently arrived American girl in London, a sketch artist seems brilliant and even tho I can hardly understand anything he says, he seems like a really nice guy. Eric is a gentle lad, slight of build with a face like a puppy that makes me smile. It's fun being together so before long we are an 'item'.

I gallivant through the sweatshop community in east London selling his designs, oblivious to the plight of the factory workers. The styles are awful. Little puffed sleeves here, a frilly pocket there, a scooped neckline with fake lace trim. But the designs sell because there is a market in London for cheap polyester dresses in the early 1970s.

Eric also paints giant self-portraits and caricatures of his father in the bathroom/studio of our West Hampstead flat. The bathroom has a lion-clawed tub, a sink, a toilet, an overstuffed chair, an easel, and all of his paints, plus a little box to put ten pence into, which gives us heat for an hour so we don't freeze to death. It is cool and very '70s to bathe while he paints and we exchange hits on Buddha sticks. We are happy enough until the day I am run out of town by the Workers Revolutionary Party.

The WRP is the actors' branch of a Trotskyist union—a group of actors I perform with in the UK led by Corin and Vanessa Redgrave. We tour factories, performing plays aimed at inspiring employees to join unions for the promise of a better life. We hand out leftist pamphlets and harass conservative-looking people in the street. I am delighted to be performing with notables like the Redgraves, but my acting involvement with WRP does not extend to being party to their political leanings. They do not like that one bit. I will not join their party, so when several members arrive at our flat, one pointing a gun, saying that I know too much about the party not to join and that I am either with them or against them—it is time to get out of Dodge.

We move to an old houseboat called *Bella* on the Prinsengracht canal in Amsterdam. My friend Siva, whom Eric and I had met years prior in London and shared a house with in Bounds Green, now lives on the canal and has invited us to stay. *Bella* is small and dilapidated with no running water or heat. But it does have an extra bed, and in 1975 it is all we need.

The nearby Melkweg is the local drug center: a huge building that offers a restaurant, a tearoom, and a multitude of events. Here it is legal to smoke pot, though other drugs are also ingested here. This is where I get a job teaching theater. It is a trip—literally—trying to get druggies to focus long enough to create anything that resembles a scene. The work also involves my touring youth centers in Holland to work with alcoholic teens. They usually throw beer bottles at me on the first day, which I turn into a game, and then they decide that improvisation is fun and look forward to my visits. It is fascinating, and rewarding, to watch these kids go from lost and despondent to hopeful and empowered through their involvement with theater and games. I feel empowered too by doing something positive in the world.

Why, then, did Eric and I move to the south of France after a delightful few years in Amsterdam reveling in the art, the canals, the outdoor markets, and the aged Gouda cheese? Because Siva decided to return to his hometown of Singapore and we had to move off the boat. He had chosen to make the voyage riding a big black three-gear Dutch bicycle. His year-long route would take him through the south of France, and I wanted to be there to greet him as he came through.

So Eric and I move south to Célony and Lisa joins us. And now she is greeting our Scandinavian buddies, who are all drug addicts from my Amsterdam days at the Melkweg. They think I will be just the right person to live with once they're out of rehab, so they arrive at my doorstep unannounced.

When a heroin addict is released from rehab, they seem to want one of three things: to get a hit of the drug, to commit suicide, or to try to stay clean but with little hope of it. At least that's what it seems like for these fellows. I immediately get them all jobs on a nearby farm, thinking that hard, backbreaking work will leave them too exhausted at the end of the day to want anything other than a hot meal and a comfortable bed. It works to a degree but overseeing this bunch takes its toll on me, leaving me depleted, and I am happy when after a month they move on.

• • •

When the kitchen is dripping with cherry syrup, it needs my full attention. It seems that everything needs my full attention—I'm feeling overwhelmed while living in paradise. During the week I work down the road at a large olive oil and wine dispensary. Humongous vats pump out the oil or wine via hoses that are used to fill empty bottles. The work is fun and it introduces me to people in my small community. Evenings, I stitch together patchwork tablecloths to sell at the famous Aix-en-Provence market each weekend. Eric contributes small pieces of wood with tiny paintings on them. Hundreds of people come through the market, and although it's enjoyable, it's draining to peddle wares all day. Any extra time I have is used to write and rehearse theatrical endeavors with Lisa. Somehow, between Lisa, Eric, and me, we scrape together enough to live on.

When Lisa gets an offer for a "real job" back in Paris, she leaves. I decide to return to Amsterdam because my relationship with Eric no longer holds interest for me and I am determined to pursue theater. We part amicably. I have no idea what I will do in Amsterdam or where I will live since Siva and his houseboat are no longer an option, but off I go, again, into the *now* confident that something will turn up. And yet another chapter in life opens like a new landscape before me. Stepping into each new unknown builds my character and strengthens my ability to walk through life with courage- scared as hell but undeterred.

Questions

- When did you step into an unknown situation?
- How did that feel?
- Why did you do it?
- What did you learn from it?

9

THE FREEZER

It is 1978. I am in my twenties and living just forty-five minutes outside Paris in Melun, a lovely rural village, with my infant son, Thomas, and my partner and great love, Yuma. We moved here in late November shortly after Thomas was born to raise him in the countryside. The beautiful two-story stone house has tiled floors, windows with shutters, and ivy along the ancient walls that surround the house and gardens. It is a dream come true, a perfect French country home, save one thing: it is freezing. In fact, in the village this house is known as "La Glacière" (the freezer). There is no central heating, and the few radiators will explode if we turn them on, so we use a single fireplace in the living room for warmth. No one mentioned the heating when we rented the house, of course, and now it's too late to do anything about it.

During the day, I dress Thomas in his snuggly and walk with him in the winter sunshine, staying out for as long possible since it's warmer outside than in the house. I whisper to my tiny son, *"Remember the wooded paths, the sound of snow crackling underfoot, the scent of wet leaves. Learn to love nature and the glow of the fireplace."* I tell him he can do anything and he will always feel loved, hoping the messages will penetrate into the fabric of his being.

Though his cheeks are permanently red from the cold, Thomas is robust and healthy. I am slender and constantly shiver, so I wash diapers by hand and iron them to get a bit of warmth. I am alone all day. There is no one to turn to for answers or help with my little boy. But there is a sturdy joy in that aloneness because it is pregnant with the purpose of motherhood: breastfeeding, protection, diaper changes.

Once daily a rural bus comes to the village to pick up or drop off anyone who needs to do an errand in another town. The big social gathering is the weekly outdoor market, bustling with vendors of fresh fruits and vegetables, fresh goat and other delectable cheeses, iron pots and pans, and an assortment of household items and clothing. The one café/bar in the tiny town is filled with smoke and crusty old men slowly sipping their apéritifs. Tending my infant requires all my time and energy, so apart from the market and the occasional villager I meet on my walks, I have little contact with the outside world.

Early every morning Yuma departs by car to the train destined for Paris, where he teaches aikido. As the day stretches toward evening, I long for his return so I can share my discoveries about the many changes I see in our infant son. There are so many things I don't know about tending to a baby, and I am consumed by my solitude.

Though I crave a word from him, Yuma never calls during the day. But he returns in the evening in time for dinner and we spend a few hours together before bed. He often pores over his books on astrology, tarot, the Kabbalah. His biggest love is stories of the Native American Indians, their warrior spirit and their communion with Mother Earth. Often, I am already exhausted from nursing, tending to our son, and the cold, and I drift off to sleep before he finishes telling me stories of his day in the big city.

Questions:

- Can you think of a time you felt responsible but unprepared for something?
- What was it and how did it feel to be in that position?
- How did you handle the situation?
- Was the outcome positive, negative or unresolved?
- Looking back, how do you feel about it now?

10

LOVE WITH BLINDERS

Yuma, a bittersweet messenger in my life. One glimpse of him dancing in Amstelpark in Amsterdam several years before, when I returned there from southern France, had sent an electric current up my spine. He was younger than I and naïve in the ways of women, but that day we began a journey as soul mates.

For years I believed a soul mate was the person you're destined to be with, twin hearts joined in perfect love. Now I know it is the person with whom you travel to hell and back, leaving no cell in your body, no bit of DNA un-scorched.

Yuma is Flemish and an aikido protégé. He is having a prolonged adventure away from his Japanese master in Paris, Noro, who will never forgive him for leaving because in Japan no one leaves the master in search of themselves and the world. Yuma is in Amsterdam performing in a troupe led by a gay, black ex–Alvin Ailey dancer, Babachu, who had seen him in Paris and lured him away to dance in his group.

Longhaired and bare chested, Yuma moves gracefully in my direction as part of a dance sequence in the park as I take my daily walk. He is wearing long beads around his neck and a piece of Balinese cloth wrapped around his waist like a skirt. He looks like a god. I snap a photo of him, thinking, *I am going to be with this guy.* A few hours later, I am.

Babachu sees the instant attraction between us and invites me to join the group. It was like that in the '70s. You could just meet someone, fall instantly in love, no questions asked, and be together. That was us.

We break into a derelict building on a forsaken Amsterdam street and squat for months while performing in festivals all over Holland, learning to love one another. I am smitten. Deeply. He is so cute, so fun and serious at the same time; he loves Bob Marley and stories about the Native Americans. He is curious, with an infectious smile and a sense of mischief.

Yuma brings me armloads of flowers he picks in other people's gardens, makes me dinners of granola because he has no idea how to cook, and instructs me in the basics of aikido. He introduces me to Buddhism and brings me with him to a Zen center in the Black Forest in Germany to work with Graf Karlfried Dürckheim, the already aged master who introduced Zen meditation to the Western world.

Yuma spends hours reading anything esoteric and sharing ideas with me. This is thrilling, new, intelligent, fun, and oh, so compelling. So when I realize that his extended bathroom trips in the middle of the night are to couple with one of the other dancers, a beautiful Israeli woman, I convince myself that it is okay. *He is younger and needs to explore. I need to be more accepting.* After all, it is the '70s, with free love and all that. I will do anything to be with him—even tolerate a breaking heart.

• • •

Then, our small apartment is ransacked by junkies, who destroy everything we own.

Oh, this is a great cosmic message, I reason, *a new beginning. Time to move back to Paris.*

We beg friends for a few clothing donations, muster up a positive outlook, and tell ourselves we will enjoy the road ahead.

In retrospect I can see that the burglary was also a sign for me to pay attention to some things about our relationship—especially Yuma's interest in other women. I convinced myself that the move to Paris would solve this problem. But being so in love at the time, I was able to disregard even this, the largest of red flags.

• • •

We arrive in Paris with nothing but the clothes on our backs and with great resolve. Lisa has an extra room in her apartment and allows us to stay there until we find a place of our own. Yuma looks forward to returning to his teacher. It is no small reunion. Master Noro did not take lightly that his protégé had left for Holland without warning one day. When he returns eighteen months later with a girlfriend, Noro takes him back, but reluctantly. He will not speak to Yuma for months, and he refuses to give him the well-earned *hakama*, the ceremonial aikido garment, until he feels Yuma had paid an emotional price for his desertion. My sweetheart returns home in tears at night, frustrated and angry at his master, who seems not to understand his need to widen his world.

It hurts to see him like that, but we find comfort in the great Parisian ice cream parlors gorging on Café Leigeois and Poire Belle Helene. We live hand to mouth in a tiny studio on an allowance from Yuma's father and the money I make managing a little shop that sells my father's line of costume jewelry sent from his office in New York. Our place is a sweet second-floor walk-up in Pigalle, an inexpensive section of Paris where one can find prostitutes, Arabs, and couscous restaurants. Over time I learn how to negotiate the customs of the area and a few Arabic words of greeting that I offer to the many men who hang out on the street there. I had been fearful of their leers and catcalls at first, but my greetings soon converted them. Now they are my protectors, making sure I get home safely from my evening escapades when Yuma is otherwise occupied.

I study aikido with Noro too, and I also spend weeks in the Black Forest of Germany with Dürkheim studying

Zen Buddhism. It is a rich time of learning that opens me to a spiritual world and much introspection.

Then I get sick. Exhausted, unable to function. Yuma reacts badly, accusing me of trying to hold him back by being sick.

"I need space to meditate and live on my own. I want you to go."

"What, now? When I'm sick?"

"I won't help you, so you better find another place."

I am baffled. *What have I done to deserve being put out like this?* I wonder. *He'll come to his senses*, I conclude. *He'll realize how much I mean to him.* I ache with longing while feeling progressively sicker each day.

The doctors I visit all have different reasons for my condition. *It is colitis. No, it is an intestinal worm.* Finally, after I have taken homeopathic remedies for weeks that do nothing, a friend takes me to a healer who declares my situation is a negative energy needing to be exorcised. He sends me to a toothless old woman with straggly gray hair, a priestess. She has constructed a ring of grasses, herbs, and who knows what else and set it ablaze, and she makes me stand in the middle of this smoking pyre. I give her the photograph of myself she requires so she can chant incantations afterward to dispel the energies that are attacking me—to call out the devil.

But the devil doesn't budge. Yuma grows colder.

"Okay, okay, I'm going. My train to Brittany leaves in the morning. I got into a theater group. I hope you're happy now."

And off I go, shattered, suitcase in hand, put out of my home so Yuma can get his space and more time for meditation without the distractions of a relationship. Or so he says. The image of other women taking my place in the apartment is constant in my mind, as is a nagging feeling I've been lied to.

Yuma

Questions:

- What was the first time you had your heart broken in a relationship?
- What did you feel like and how did it affect your life?
- Were there red flags in the relationship that you dismissed?

- Do you recognize red flags now that you didn't then?
- Has that changed how you interact in relationships now? How?

11

DIAGNOSIS

My new digs in Saint-Brieuc, Brittany, are in a huge empty brick schoolhouse where we will begin rehearsals. The former schoolroom that is my bedroom has a mattress on the floor, a box for personal items, and a string stretched across the room from which my few clothes will hang. The whole place echoes. With every sound, every creak, the whistling of the wind through the cracked windows, my body stiffens in fear: I have visions of someone coming out of the shadows to hack me to death. The empty schoolyard sports no joyful cries of children playing. There is just the eerie quiet of loneliness. I am nauseous all the time and grief stricken. Every day it feels like I'm going through the motions of being alive. Inside me, everything is flat and gray.

After a few days of rehearsals, the theater director notices that I'm not eating, and he sends me to a doctor he knows. Monsieur le médecin takes one look at me and puts a stethoscope to my belly.

"*Vous entendez le petit chou-chou? C'est votre Bébé.*"

Colitis? Intestinal worms, exorcism? *Oh, please!* I'm pregnant.

I'm both terrified and elated by the reality of a new life within me. I hide my condition from the troupe for as long as possible for fear of being fired, but must run off the stage often to throw up. They know ... and they're okay with it.

Yuma never comes to see me. Not once. He is too busy meditating on Beatrice—the real reason behind his sudden meanness. But when he finally earns his *hakama*, his parents, unaware we've broken up, invite me to the celebration in Paris.

No invitation comes from Yuma, but I decide to go anyway. *Maybe when he sees me,* I think, *he'll suddenly realize his stupidity in sending me away.* But when the train pulls into the Gare du Nord, I see him in the distance kissing Beatrice. He turns and walks toward me.

"*Why do you have to be with another woman right before coming to get me?*"

"*Why don't you get on de train and go back where you came from?*"

"*Because I'm pregnant—with your baby!*"

Stone silence.

Then: "*I can't dink of anyone who would be a beder modder for my child. I will cudit off wid Beatrice right away.*"

It's a miracle. We resume our life together, every past hurt forgotten. We get our place in Melun to create a home for when the baby is born. We live there for a couple of months as a family. One day I am warming myself and my infant son by the fire in the big cold house, and I notice a note Yuma had left me before his morning departure:

Sweet Diane,

I am going to live in Germany where I will be teaching aikido in a dojo built for me there by Durkheim. I love you but cannot do this life together. I had to choose between my God and my blood. I choose God. I hope you will find it in your heart to pack and send my things, but if not, I will do without. I know you will make a fine mother and will manage.

Good luck,
Yuma

. . .

For the following week, I limp along from one day to the next, trying to make sense of things. *What do I do? Where do I go? How will I manage with Thomas by myself?* Then Dürckheim sends word that I should go La Sainte-Baume, where he has arranged for a position for me.

La Sainte-Baume is a spiritual/cultural center run by Dominican priests that sits on a plateau above Marseilles in southern France. It is known as a place of pilgrimage to Mary Magdalene, whose relics are contained in a chapel in the mountains here. With Thomas strapped to my back, I work in the kitchen and the gift shop and offer dance classes to guests. We have a small room with a wooden floor where my little son sleeps on an assortment of floor pillows and I on a cot. We spend our rare free time hiking through the glorious surroundings, listening for Gregorian chants wafting up from cave dwellings where hermits live, and crossing paths with guests who have come to make pilgrimage.

People are kind, but no one offers to help me with my child. It is tough to work while attending to an infant and warding off exhaustion and the pain of abandonment, all in order to present an air of good spiritedness to my baby and the world. But it is a safe place and a good place, and I am grateful to be here for now.

When the center's high season ends, there is no more work for me. But through divine intervention and one of the guests at La Sainte-Baume, I land a job with a dance group headed for Salernes, another small town in the south. During rehearsals Thomas sits on a blanket gumming a crust of baguette. When he crawls toward me, another dancer scoops him up and places him back on the blanket. It is a sweet time of community and respite from my isolation. I find the rehearsals exhilarating because dancing always nourishes my spirit.

But I never get to perform with the group. Yuma's letter arrives a few weeks in. He is settled in Germany now, he says, and he wants us to be a family again. *Be still my heart. My love is coming to get me!* The anguish of the past is forgotten in a flash of youthful naïveté. Well, and desperation. I simply pack my bags and wait, happy to be heading back to Todtmoos.

Questions

- Have you ever had turnaround in your life that caused you to accept something that had previously hurt you?
- Describe what hurt you and how you managed to dismiss the hurt?
- Why did you do that?

12

ZEN

I had first visited there several years prior, when Yuma and I went to spend ten days at Dürckheim's Zen community. We were young and in love, and he was excited to introduce me to the center but especially to his mentor.

"We vill stay in the big house dis time. Dere is a goot room dere, and it is where we take our meals."

I listened to the music of Yuma's thick Flemish accent as my eyes inhaled the landscape with delight. We wound our way to the tiny mountain community on narrow roads lined with wild daisies and poppies. It was refreshing to be in nature, away from the hustle and bustle of our little Paris apartment.

"What will we do there every day?"

"We medidate first ting ehvree morning. Dere is a little cabin we walk to for de five a.m. sessions. Dürckheim is always dere and gifes a little talk after the medidation. Den we go to breakfast at de big house. It is always big slabs of cheese, black bread, and goot coffee. Den you can plan your day as you wish. Do walking medidations, art classes, horseback riding, or just hang out. You will also haf private sessions with Dürckheim."

"Horseback riding?"

"Well, yea. Dere are lots of actifities but dey all center around the hara breath. So you do everyding as a medidative practice; even horse riding."

"And what are the sessions with Dürkcheim like?"

"You'll zee. You ask too many questions."

The driveway to the Todtmos community was a long dusty dirt road leading to a parking area near a large wood-and-stucco central building. Smaller homes surrounding the building were scattered about the hilly property. The structures all looked solidly built for cold mountain winters. But my first visit was on a warm summer day, and the buildings gave a sense of weight to the place.

Walking paths were everywhere, leading from house to house and into the hills. People on those paths walked very slowly, as though carrying a big load, looking at their feet. They seemed to be reflecting on the sadness and toil of life. But I felt bubbly and wondered if my joyful exuberance would clash with the heavy, methodical, German energy of this place.

As soon as we entered the Grosses Haus (Big House), we were met by Frau Adele, a neat and tidy woman of short stature and strong will. As the house mother, she oversaw meal times, guest conduct, house cleanliness, and silence. Unsmiling and with a tight bun at the nape of her neck, she showed us to our room as she informed us of the house rules, of which there were many. Meal times, quiet times, cleaning times, times we were and were not allowed in the main building, rules for the shared bathroom, no food in the rooms. And of course no hanky-panky. This is a place of spiritual retreat.

Ooohhhh yes. I think my rebellious nature is going to clash with this environment.

We settled into the spacious room, putting our meager belongings into drawers and stashing the bags, careful not to make a mess in case Frau Adele wandered in for a tidiness inspection. Then we headed down to the dining hall for a lunch of pea soup, thick slices of black bread, aged Gouda cheese, and apples. Perfect grounding food.

Dürckheim's house was warm and welcoming, with an Asian touch—sparse, with every piece placed in a manner that gave it value. Big, cushy chairs, Japanese paintings, and soft colors. When we met Dürckheim, he took my hand in both of his and held it there, as if exchanging energy with me—or getting a sense of mine. The gesture immediately opened my heart; he felt like a grandfather to me. After the exchange of a few niceties—*"How was your trip? Have you found your room? Did you have a good lunch?"*—he inquired about my interests in Todtmoos.

I had no idea other than to discover the many ways to exercise the *hara*, the point below the navel that is the spiritual/energetic center. It was to be the focus of my breath at all times, and I could learn to do this through art, movement, horseback riding, Zen meditation, and more. I wanted to explore it all.

I felt so much warmth in his presence. In his late seventies, he had an oblong face, a pronounced nose, thinning hair, and liver spots on his hands. His English was good and he spoke slowly, informing me that we would meet a few more times during our stay. During one of these meetings Dürckheim looked at the lines in the palm of my hand and explained that the star pattern in the center indicated I possessed an enormous capacity for love. I believed this would see me through every challenge in my life.

This Zen master was a solid mentor with whom I felt seen and loved. He was authentic, and I felt warm and safe in his presence. A psychotherapist and veteran of World War II, he had been introduced to Zen Buddhism as a young man. He created Todtmoos much later in life as a community for the purpose of teaching practices leading to self -realization. Working with Dürckheim was like plunging into an abyss where everything I thought was real was being scrutinized and the fields between the spiritual and mundane were melting.

When Dürkheim gave me a copy of his book, *Dialogue sur le Chemin Initiatique*, I was thrilled. He signed it "*Diane, je vous accompagne*" (I accompany you). The book introduced me to zazen.

Every morning at 5:00, Yuma and I walked over to the dojo for a group mediation led by Dürckheim, who sometimes fell asleep. Initiates walked around the room with long sticks they used to awaken us should we, too, slip into a nap.

Every one-on-one meeting with Dürckheim in his room seemed like an amiable chit-chat, my hand in his. He was curious about my life with Yuma, my interests and aspirations. He talked about hara breathing and encouraged me to pay special attention to that during my stay. When I left his room, my entire body vibrated as if charged with an electric current. Whatever he was doing while innocently holding my hand in his, I liked it, and I looked forward to more time with him.

On that first day in Todtmoos, I explored the compound. People seemed to be working hard at being attentive to their hara. The energy was so different from in France, where people eagerly kissed one another on each cheek upon meeting. Here, eyes were cast downward as people moved ponderously around the grounds, as though studying every step. No one smiled. I vowed to stir up some fun. *Why not? I can be spiritual and still have fun!*

A sense of deep contentment expanded within me as I wandered up the logging road that took me into the mountains. From that vantage point I could feast my eyes upon vast prairies of arnica, bluebells, and buttercups. Yuma had disappeared into his own activities: painting, meditating, in the library studying tarot, astrology, or the Kabbalah. He was a strict teacher in his aikido classes, which I attended, but we enjoyed our walk to the morning meditations, meeting for meals, and sharing the adventures of our day each evening while cuddling in bed.

I drew big black circles with ink and a thick sumi brush in my art class. The spontaneity of the movement, direction of the circle, thickness of the lines, roundness of the form: all these reflected my inner workings, my challenges, and my relationship with myself. I had to make a lot of circles before I was satisfied. Frustration set in quickly because I could not make what happened on the paper look like what was in my head. Inner voices blasted my incompetence, stupidity, lack of creativity. More circles, more circles, each pushing past the voices toward liberation. My patient, kind, but firm teacher repeated, *"Focus on the hara. Let the movement come from there."*

In my attempt at working with clay I discovered that I abhorred the sensation of slimy, slippery mud in my hands. I was taught that this aversion indicated a poor relationship with my mother. I knew this was correct. Deeply uncomfortable things about myself were emerging. *Am I turning into one of those morose-looking people wandering all over this place?* I wondered.

Dürckheim gave me permission to teach movement from the hara. My technique was slow-motion movement but still fun because it was expressive. I preferred relating to the upbeat, sociable parts of myself and tried to ignore my vulnerable and more challenging aspects.

I baked little cakes and started tea-time gatherings to inspire a sense of lightness at the center. This was not exactly the point of Todtmoos. It was more a place of deep introspection, but Dürckheim didn't try to stop me. He seemed amused by my machinations and graciously accepted my little cakes. I was struggling emotionally but also compelled to do the work of knowing and improving myself.

I really did have a problem with my mother and, like her, I could easily fall into a victim mentality, and I liked to keep busy to avoid the discomfort of prolonged silence. I was not confident with my being-ness, so doing-ness became my m.o.

Yuma challenged me by bringing up the underbelly of my personality. In aikido he criticized me. When we were on hikes he would laugh at my fear of being stranded in the forest—and then disappear. He went through my astrological chart pointing out all the things I needed to change. There was plenty of love, enjoyment and fun. We danced like maniacs in our bedroom to Stevie Wonder tunes, he loved showing me new hikes and surprising me with delicious patisseries. We spent hours chatting about new observations but his criticisms nestled into my being as triggers to larger issues from my past. His charm was undeniable but like maman, he could turn it on an off always keeping me off balance.

Questions:

- When did you notice things about yourself that were painful or embarrassing?
- Did you try and keep them hidden or did you try and work with your issues? How?

- Were you ever with a partner who triggered a feeling of smallness in you?
- What was the trigger?
- How did you handle that?
- Looking back, how do you feel about that now?

13

A ROOM NEAR THE KITCHEN

Now, several years later, after Yuma had left me stranded with an infant and a scrap of paper telling me I'd be fine, he and I and our son would be together again. I was overjoyed to be returning to Todtmoos with him. The journey to Dürckheim's place in Yuma's little white Toyota was glorious, Isaiah gurgling happily as we feasted on beautiful scenery, catching up with one another and singing songs. It was the first time in months that peace was in my heart. I was so happy. We were almost there when Yuma said:

"By de way, dere is a room for you and Thomas on de far side of the house near the kitchen."

"What do you mean?"

"*Renate and Thom are my girlfriends dere. Renate is an older voman and very nice. Thom is younger den you. She gets jealous and can be a pain but I dink you vill like her. I don't vant us to live in de same room.*"

"*You mean we are not going to live as a family?*"

"*I vill never spend de whole night with you. Women can suck de energy of a man. I vant to be around my son. Dere is no reason to be jealous. Dat is a stupid emotion.*"

The pain of betrayal and powerlessness is unbearable. For the next month tears of frustration and anger fueled my every waking moment. Yuma wanted someone who would cook, sew, and attend to his son and I was just his ticket to that. When we fought he retreated to one of his women. I was left in never-ending misery.

I will go to Durkheim, I decided. *He loves me and I know he will help.* He held my hand as I sobbed, gave me tissues and did not interrupt. As a seasoned psychotherapist he knew exactly how to handle this. He also understood that one must face one's challenges and grow from them. He did not approve of Yuma's actions, but he saw his young student's incredible talent and charisma in teaching aikido, and he encouraged me to adapt, meditate, breathe, and let things unfold organically. He did not tell me what to do other than that.

I tried to accept things as they were. I really tried.

After a month of torment, I packed a bag, put Thomas in a snuggly, and set off to walk out of Todtmoos without a word to anyone. My brilliant plan was to walk to Belgium with my child on my back and take a plane back to the States. *When life becomes unbearable, just pack your bags and leave.*

On my way out of the compound I crossed paths with Renate, Yuma's older girlfriend. I shared my misery with her and told her I was leaving. Her compassionate response was to go into her house and return with the keys to Yuma's car. *"Take his car. You cannot walk. I will deal with him later."*

So I drove to Belgium, where Yuma's parents reluctantly bought me a one-way ticket to America. Thomas was ten months old. My sister had sent a telegram saying, *"Come home to where people love you. You need taking care of."*

I never went back to Todtmoos or communicated with Dürckheim again. His dedications in the books he gave me are precious, as is the indelible mark he made on my life. My love for him never changed. He died a few years after I left Todtmoos. But death doesn't change the memory of love, and I have the memory.

I did not recognize it at the time but later realized that our universe is compassionate because it repeats our challenges until we truly understand the lesson we are supposed to learn. Red flags in relationships do not go away when we ignore them. They need to be dealt with.

Questions:

- Please describe a situation where you felt betrayed.
- What actions did you take to protect yourself?
- How did that work out and how did it help you make better decisions now?

14

To Amherst

I was twenty-eight years old when I arrived in Amherst, Massachusetts, with my son. I barely spoke for the first year of the twenty years I lived there. I had a will to survive and to provide a safe place for my son, but I had no words feeling numb, exhausted and despondent. Several years later I had a second son, Michael, from yet another failed relationship, and made a life for all of us.

After spending the first few days with my sister, it became clear to me that the warm welcome into her loving home I'd imagined had been a pipe dream. It was obvious that my baby and I were an imposition, so an isolated, creaky farmhouse five miles outside of town became home. There was no heat. There were huge drafts. The floorboards were slanted and the water pipes froze, but it was ours for the winter. I arranged for food stamps, received clothes from the community survival center, and hitchhiked into town for groceries. We were cold. Again. And alone. But we never got sick that winter, and when the snow melted the glorious sound of cicadas comforted us.

While living in the farmhouse, I endured an all-consuming sensation, a pulling apart in my solar plexus. It was as if the molecules were coming undone from that part of my body and my life force was draining out. Often, in the depths of despondency, I felt a hand reaching through my skull and grabbing my spinal column to keep me upright, walking me around like a puppet. *Where did this arm, this force come from that keeps me from totally dissolving? What keeps me standing and moving forward when death seems a welcome alternative?*

I felt untethered, floating and deeply vulnerable. It was scary so isolated in the big house , dirt poor, without a car or neighbors close by. I was fearful in my great aloneness and the notion that I could not survive on my own. Every little creak made me jump. Yet I had a toddler to care for and a strong desire not to project upon him the inner demons of my spirit. I pretended to be strong to keep going.

I am a spiral unfolding in space
My body contained in the movement
From earth to heaven
Held together in the eye of the tornado.
Sometimes I am lost

And from that brewing place
A part of me gets cast out
Perhaps my arm or foot or mind
Orbiting in space and time
Searching for itself

How do you bring back into the fold
A heart and spirit smashed and forlorn?
It clunks within the spinning that surrounds it
Like an old fork that has found its way to the
Bottom of the dishwasher in the spin cycle.

Questions:

- What was a situation that left you feeling bereft and hopeless?
- At that point what did you do?
- How did you soldier on despite being depleted?
- What have you learned about working through your emotions?

15

A REVELATION

After surviving winter in the farmhouse, I find an apartment in family housing. My neighbors are a lovely Nigerian family with three daughters, one of whom, Modupeore, is Thomas's age. They go to school together and I love her. But after years of relocations, we lose track of one another—until thirty-five years later while we are both living in California, she shows up on Facebook.

After so many years it's thrilling to plan a visit in Oakland, where my youngest brother, James, also lives. Modupeore is a musician and married to a sweet white fellow. During the visit we discover many similarities in our lives despite the difference in our ages: our healthy eating habits, our spiritual inclinations, our love of travel and of people. It is during our conversation about spirituality that Dürckheim comes up.

"*Well, my first real introduction to spirituality was zazen,*" I tell her. "*I studied with an old man in Germany whose name was Karlfried Dürckheim. He was an amazing person, warm and loving. He was like a sweet grandfather to me, but much more than that. He taught me another way to see the world, how to meditate, and so much more. I have his books.*"

Modupeore's husband interjects.

"*I know of that guy. My mother studied Zen and heard of him years ago. He was a Nazi.*"

"*Wh–what?*" I sputter. "*No, it can't be the same person. That is not possible. Dürckheim was a great human being. Not a Nazi.*"

"*Yes, he was. It is the same person. He was very high up in the party and close to Hitler. His job was to spread Nazi propaganda to the people. But it turns out his great-grandmother was Jewish so the Nazis were embarrassed and didn't know what to do with him. So they sent him to Japan. Look it up on the Internet. There is a lot of information there.*"

Frozen in utter disbelief, I cannot integrate this information. *How could Dürckheim have been a Nazi? How can I have loved and felt so loved by . . . a Nazi?* The information stirs chaos within me. It's like a dagger in my heart.

I must do some research. Modupeore's husband is full of shit! This is like entertaining the idea that your husband is a pedophile or your child is a mass murderer.

It is true, though, I learn. My grandfatherly mentor had once been a prominent member of the Nazi Party.

I comb through his books looking for a word, a sign that he had repented for the error of his ways, that he had a great spiritual awakening and regretted his previous actions. Nothing. Not one word of remorse or even acknowledgment. It is as if he just shed that persona like a snake sheds its outer skin. And the more I read, the more similarities I can see between the Nazi Party and the Zen Buddhist mentality of Japan during that time, which espoused support for Japanese nationalism and militarism.

But Zen is a practice of meditation to deepen the association with a life force that transcends the ego and solidifies a rapport with the oneness of all things. The practice Dürckheim developed—partially from his association with spiritual leaders in Japan after being sent there by the Nazis—as well as his work in psychotherapy seemed to directly oppose his work with the Nazi Party. That he would never revisit or even refer to that time after returning to Germany in 1947 is an enigma.

I struggle deeply with this revelation, but I also realize that many persons of spirit have transcended a past filled with horror. Milarepa was such a personality. Now known as one of Tibet's most famous, beloved yogis and poets, his past included training in sorcery and black magic, which he used to destroy villages and crops and commit vengeful killings, before transcending these acts and attaining enlightenment. Still this reality about Durkheim feels like a knife being twisted in my solar plexus. *How could I have not known? How could such a good person have been a Nazi? My heart was so open to him. What does that say about me?*

The paradoxes in everyday life abound. We are called upon to make sense of a world filled with opposing factors. Our political system promises the protection and safety of the people. We want to trust it, and we want the individuals we vote for to honor their roles, but time and time again we are confronted with corruption and the demise of what we hold dear. Seemingly loving parents abuse their children. Religious leaders molest their parishioners. And the man who touched my soul was a Nazi. I hold this within myself as a suspended breath: that rollover place between the inhalation and the exhalation. An unfathomable schism I may never be able to fully cross.

Questions:

- What has been the biggest shock you have felt about a person that you thought you knew?
- Describe your reactions to this.
- How did it affect your life then?
- How do you feel about it now?

16

SWEET MURIELLE

That is the name given to my older sister by my paternal grandmother, who has no idea she is being conned into giving her money, dresses, and preferential treatment. I sense that something is amiss with my sister.

I would love to have someone to cuddle with in bed, sipping cups of tea and talking about my latest crush or my first kiss. Instead my sister does her best to seduce every single one of my boyfriends with her boobs and promises of sex. She is beautiful, smart, and talented and I look to her for girlish guidance and inspiration. Instead of providing it, she devises ways to leave me feeling small and hurt. When she silently slides over to my bed at night as I am deep in sleep, bringing her head close to my ear and yelling, "*Boo!*" my tears amuse her.

So I am beyond excited when suddenly Sweet Murielle invites me to visit her at Fisher College in Boston her freshman year. This, I am certain, signals her recognition of me as an asset and a cool little sister.

She greets me with a kiss at the bus stop and announces the day's adventures. I can hardly believe my luck. Walking down Beacon Street with my big sister is exhilarating. We enter a shop where the older sales woman greets her by name. I feel so grown up.

In and out of the dressing room she goes, trying on skirts, blouses, and sweaters until she finally decides upon only one purchase, a blue shirt. She is charming to the sales lady. On the way home she is elated.

"*Stupid old bat. She couldn't even see what was happening right in front of her face. Serves her right.*"

Under her coat is an entire new outfit stolen from right under the nose of the trusting saleswoman. "*Serves her right*" is a phrase I hear throughout our lifetime: when she steals money from our parents, sneaks boys into the dorm through the window, or milks the system for money by getting on welfare when she is perfectly capable of working. If I confront her, she flies into a white rage. But when I receive her letter in Europe at a desperately low point in my life, promising to take care of me, I believe.

"*Come back, come back to where you are loved and people can take care of you,*" her letter says. "*Come to Amherst. I will be here for you.*"

So I return to the USA, downtrodden, disillusioned, and heartbroken from my split with Yuma, with Thomas on my back and everything I can carry in a suitcase.

I am exhausted from a long flight when we land in Boston. Thomas had cried the entire time, in pain from an ear infection I was not aware of. Passengers seemed ready to strangle me, but what could I do? It is midnight and the airport banks are closed so I only have French francs. Thomas is in a snuggly with a wet diaper and my arms are full with everything I can carry. *Oh, please. Somebody help me.* Here I am again, feeling abandoned.

My head cranes to look left, then right, then left, then right. Over and over again. Until I realize that nobody is coming to get me. Sweet Murielle has stood me up. My insides are churning in utter disbelief. I am exhausted and despondent but I have to carry on.

"You absolutely have to take me to the Greyhound station. You cannot leave a woman with a baby all alone in the airport. I can only give you French money, but you have to do this."

And by some miracle, for a handful of French francs the taxi driver takes me. Then the bus driver does the same, only this time I have no francs left. He does it out of the goodness of his heart, or out of pity, or to shut me up. And at 5 a.m. I arrive in Amherst, Massachusetts, at my sister's doorstep, a big hocking mess.

"Why didn't you come to get me?"

"I was busy. And I knew you would manage."

WTF? I want to slug her but don't because I am afraid she will tell me to go elsewhere and I have nowhere to go.

I am beyond tired, angry with an infant on my back and I cannot believe I have allowed myself to be sucker-punched by my sister… again. Neverthless,

"I'm starving."

"Okay, let me get you a rice cake."

It takes only a week for me to realize that the living arrangement is impossible. My sister is still the same person I knew as a child. Nothing has changed. I feel so manipulated and stupid for having fallen for her antics.

"Diáne, if Thomas wakes up early please take him outside. We all need our sleep and don't want to hear him cry."

Within a few days I search for and find that old, isolated farmhouse with no heat and broken water pipes just outside of town. The rent is $100 a month. I have little money and no job. This will be our home for the winter. I have no choice. We are cold but anything is better than being at my sisters. And here I am again, desperate for a sense of security where there is none.

Over and over again, motherhood has pummeled me with opportunities to love unconditionally, to carry on past my self- perceived limitations - to maintain. Each act of maintaining builds arsenal of fortitude that keeps propelling me onward little by little. . The love of and need to protect my child is a momentous gift that has the power to move me out of my grief and into finding solutions that will keep us safe and out of the abyss of suffering even when I return to that abyss over and over again feeling like no matter what I do security will evade me. Time and time again I return to being that 7 year old girl, that abandoned new mom, that shocked disciple. Can I get a break?

Questions:

- If you have siblings, what is your relationship with them? Be specific.
- Recount a family story about an interaction with your siblings
- Did you ever find yourself in danger? Please describe the situation.
- How did you call on your inner courage during that time?
- What did you learn from it?

17

THE SNAKE PIT

It's dark in my mind. Inky black. I hate it in here where I have been before so many times. No one can help me, and no one really cares to. Nothing I have believed in and tried to do works in this place. I am overwhelmed by a sense of futility. All the stories I have been told about the goodness of humanity, all the "smile and everything will be all right" that I believed, everything I thought I could do to make my life better—I can't find it here.

I am a misfit. My idiosyncrasies are reflected everywhere. I am too sensitive, too offensive, too attached, too needy, too independent, too rigid. No matter what I do I am not good enough, big enough, understanding enough, mature enough, or whatever other enoughs I am not.

I have lost faith. I want to die, and I don't care that I want to die. There is nothing worth living for anymore. I just want to stop all the voices within me telling me that nothing will ever pan out because I will always mess things up. I can't stand being myself. There is no hope, no escape. This is hell and I don't know how to get out. Another voice calls out from within: *Something, someone please help me.*

But no one can.

This is my personal snake pit. I have been here in the deepest, darkest most hopeless times of my life when I felt betrayed by everything. I have been sucked into this pit by my childhood illness, by a narcissistic mother, by the pain of being molested, by betrayal and abandonment, by the overwhelming isolation of raising my child alone ... the list is a mile long.

This is my starting place: the exalted position of being as low as possible. It is from this place that each time, I choose to live or die—and it can go either way. I strain to find something, anything powerful enough to give me faith that life is still worth living, to help me climb out again, something to be grateful for. I always find something. I have to. Gratitude is the antidote.

Questions:

- Have you ever felt totally despondent? Please describe.
- What did you do about it?
- How did you cultivate inner resources when dealing with a dismal situation?
- How do you feel now in your life when feeling very low?

18

PARENTING ALONE

At the break of dawn I can hear the sound of little Thomas's shuffling feet pattering across the living room floor into my room. Until recently he would just creep over and breathe in my face until I opened my eyes. We are living in our rented house in Northampton, Massachusetts. *"Can I come in your bed?"*

First thing in the morning, warm, groggy, and soft, his four-year-old independent self melts into an ageless form to be stroked and cuddled. At least for five minutes or so.

Then, comes the inevitable *"I'm hungry"* as I plead for another few minutes of sleep. I know it is in vain, that he will win and get his Cheerios before I am ready or willing to get up. Then the day unfolds quickly. Suddenly we are in a hurry. But the memory and warmth linger on throughout the day, throughout a lifetime of reliving those privileged moments of love that fuel the will to live.

We thoroughly enjoy one another, Thomas and I. Mothering adds such joy and dimension to my life. He is handsome, helpful, charismatic, and empathetic as a child and young boy. There are gremlins to work out because of being deserted by his father, Yuma, but he is truly a good-natured kid and the bond between us is strong. We love discovering new places and things together, which makes it easier when five years after having Isaiah all to myself, another boy enters our family.

"*Goodnight, peanut,*" I say, bending to kiss Michael goodnight. Silence, then:

"*Goodnight, mushroom,*" he answers and to this day, words have never failed him.

His father, Daniel, and I were the first case in Massachusetts to be granted joint custody despite not being married or cohabiting. Our relationship was a brief two years and we had been estranged since my pregnancy. Michael had shuttled back and forth between us from birth, which I railed against, believing that babies needed to stay primarily with one parent. Kids like stability, and although Daniel and I lived on the same street, going back and forth would upset any child's sense of safety during his formative years.

The results manifested later as Michael acted out to such an extent that he was thrown out of every school he ever attended, including the one for at-risk children, until he quit school altogether at age sixteen.

He was cute, funny, and quick. He loved head rubs but didn't like to snuggle much. At only nine months old he was walking. At seven, after watching a Chinese circus on the television, he disappeared and came back to announce that he had learned how to pop a wheelie on his bike. Soon after, he jumped in the complex's swimming pool and picked up how to swim its length just by watching how others did it. But something always seemed to be bugging him. He needed to say no to everything, then be cajoled into trying it, only to discover that it was fun or good, be it a new food or an adventure. In school he was like a pendulum swinging back and forth between failing and the dean's list; as soon as he was able to prove his intelligence, he stopped working until he failed and then went on to prove himself again. As an adolescent he refused to get a job delivering papers or shoveling snow for pocket money yet complained when I couldn't give him money. But he always made me laugh. Each April Fool's Day he had a scheme prepared to trick me, like making me breakfast in bed but lacing it with large amounts of salt, or covering the toilet with cellophane. He would call the apartment impersonating the police, pretending he was being held and requiring me to fetch him. He made me roar with laughter by impersonating the mannerisms of my friends. Michael: full of bravado, so fragile within. He drove me crazy and I missed him terribly whenever we were separated.

Being on welfare was a humiliating necessity. Sitting in the welfare office to get food stamps, or going to the survival center to get Thanksgiving dinner and Christmas gifts for the boys: these things held such a stigma. And saying 'no, we can't afford it" to my kids so often left me feeling like a failure. But I was grateful to get help, without which we could have been homeless. When I finally got a part-time job at the Amherst Family Center, it allowed me to pay for my own food. I supplemented my income by cleaning houses—lots of them—but even cleaning toilets helped me feel infinitely better about myself as a well-traveled, educated woman from a middle-class family.

When Michael was twelve, his father died suddenly of cancer. That boy never shed a tear. Instead he begged for a television (our first) so he could watch funny movies, acted out in school, expressed disgust at everything I cooked, got into fights, and constantly challenged every house rule. It was the year from hell when I could do nothing right in his eyes and the school called me every other day to complain about his behavior. It was brutal to feel so beaten down and still be the understanding parent. I wanted to scream for it all to stop and just lock him in his room but I forced myself to take the punches and shower him with love anyway.

Thomas was different in every way. As a child he took seriously his role as older brother and adopted a positive, can-do attitude about life. He did whatever he could to help out at home and sought out little jobs in the neighborhood to earn extra money. We enjoyed many of the same things; hiking, raking leaves, snuggles. He was always there for me when life felt too hard and I was discouraged. But like most kids, he had a side that rebelled as he grew older.

As a teen Thomas and his friends rocked the house with the type of music that could only bring on a terrific migraine. Once as I climbed the steps to the kitchen with groceries in both arms and ten-year-old Michael in tow, the pungent scent of pot hit me like a wall.

I don't want them doing this in my house. C'mon, how can he not know that what they're doing is against all the rules? My rules. My house.

Bags are dumped on the table and I stomp down to the basement where they are rehearsing. It is deafening and they don't hear me coming. They should, though, because I am *roaring*.

"Get out! All of you! Get out of my house! You cannot do that here!"

The boys, all four of them, practically trip over each other to get out the door with the instruments that have been making the house shake with a deafening acid ruckus. I imagine tomorrow's local paper headline: Stoned Teenaged Boys Scared to Death by Rabid Mom.

They will never do that again or come near my house either.

Thomas is standing with a "death to Mom" look on his face. He is mortified that his mother was so tripped out.

"Well, do you want your little brother to see this shit? And open the windows. It reeks in here."

He will probably be mortified by his friends' stories at school tomorrow about his demented psycho mom. His eyes are swollen with pot smoking and the rage he can only express through stony silence.

There was a lot of rage that year, and for many years. Yuma died only six months after Daniel, and even though Yuma had no contact with Thomas, the loss was huge. Two boys, one house, dead dads, no support for me. Where did the children direct their pain? Meeeeeee—the punching bag, their voices replaying over and over again what they wanted from me that I couldn't give or didn't have. How different I was from other parents. *Sometimes only humor can save the day.*

Why can't you be looser?
Why can't you chill out?
Why do you always have to yell?
Why is the stain on the couch a big deal?
Or the broken plate, bed, futon, candleholder, computer?
Why do we need to tell you where we are?
Is there more juice?
Who asked you to work so hard?
Why can't you change your parenting skills?
You don't understand anything.
You really fucked us up.
Why do you have to worry about us?
Can we get some Pop-Tarts?
Can you give me a ride to the game?
You never do anything for us.
Any cookies left?
Mom. Did you see that?

Questions:

- Do you have children?
- What are the most memorable and challenging memories you have of them?
- How did being a parent help you to grow?
- What did you learn from your children?
- Did you learn unconditional love as a parent? How?
- What would you say to new parents?

19

AFRICA, 1986

We can't get enough of each other. Wrapped in his arms his eternal kiss in the stairwell at the NPR station causes my knees to buckle. I am drunk from the scent of him, the feel of his torso pressing against me. He isn't flustered that I have two young children, this handsome, charming Kenyan radio producer of pan-African music. I am thunderstruck. This moment, this kiss is the start of a wild, eight-year-long journey that will test and expand every aspect of my being.

I have a knack for getting passionately involved in relationships with men who have one foot out the door. But as a single mother of two, I easily dismiss red flags in relationships because the need for support and to be touched, loved, and acknowledged is so great. *I am so lucky that he even looks in my direction, for who would really want a woman with kids? Let me be grateful for whatever I can get.*

We have many things in common, including passionate love of dance and music. He teaches me to hear every individual instrument and rhythm in a piece of Latin music so as to appreciate all its subtleties, and how to distinguish music from each part of the African diaspora. He introduces me to the world of public broadcasting and is instrumental in my being hired as a producer of an NPR French-language radio show. I can hardly believe that I am being seen, and appreciated for anything outside of raising kids. This is nourishing to me, this adventure.

Suddenly my friends are international mixed-race couples, and life is vibrant, welcoming. I'm in a world of polyrhythm's that spikes my interest in a soulful connection to the continent of Africa. We organize monthly dances with African music and soulful food from Tanzania, Nigeria and Kenya and sink into one another's arms at the end of the night.

But the relationship is confusing to me, especially his relationships with other women and the resurfacing of my old patterns. *Please don't let this be just one more dead-end relationship that breaks my heart and makes me use all my strength to be strong.* Being with him is so different from what I've experienced before. *Why does he dance with all other women when we go to a club before dancing with me? Why is he always late? He seems very attracted to me but ignores me around other people, why?* I want to understand which differences are personal and which are cultural—and it gives me an idea ...

Going to Africa. Going to leave the white way far behind and move to the beat—to live this and understand.

Lots of mothers leave their children with families and go off. Mexican and Haitian moms go off to work and send money home to their families. But not many white moms like me. Years of struggling to be everything to my fatherless boys has left little time for the spirited, creative, and adventurous being I once was. No matter how much love there is, some parts just wither up.

I would be gone for five months, immersing myself in the music I had discovered thanks to my handsome Kenyan man who would become my husband. I yearned to feel, in the places of their birth, the polyrhythm's that compelled my body to dance from the depths of my soul. I would end the trip in Kenya, meeting my lover's stepmother and siblings, to better understand his birthplace too in hopes of becoming more comfortable with our relationship. But I will have to deal with leaving my children for months. *Will they forget me? Will it cause trauma? Can I do this without feeling wracked with guilt?*

I labor over these questions and finally decide to go find myself again. Thomas goes to live with my mother and Michael, my youngest son goes to live with his father who you will meet later.

On the never-ending plane ride to Senegal, I vow, *Say yes to everything, try all new things and be a gracious guest in the cultures you are about to discover. Amen.*

At the terminal heading for the exit I stop short, astounded. A group of people are standing there holding a large sign with my name on it. Everybody is grinning. They are giants: a towering group of very blue black men in floor-length robes, women in magnificent booboos and headdresses. They are the family of a U Mass student I befriended who has told them that I am coming and that they are to treat me like family. I count seventeen majestic titans who have come to greet this bedraggled five-feet-two white girl in rumpled clothes who has just traveled for more than twenty hours. I feel small, dirty, and insignificant—like a fire hydrant in comparison. It all seems unworldly, but they look excited to see me. *What on earth did my friend tell them?*

Back at their compound, a meal is prepared. *"This ezz traditional. You lak eet yes?."*

Goat curry. A gigantic bowlful with a tall glass of tap water. Suddenly I am totally not hungry.

Okay, I don't think I'm gonna die from eating meat for the first time in fifteen years, but that glass of tap water? Remember the promise, I remind myself. *Remember yes.*

Shit, there are no utensils. I have to eat with my hands. With the entirety of my new family standing expectantly in a circle around me, watching me, I fumble and then try to appear nonchalant with curry dripping down my arms. My mouth is on fire and tears are dripping down my face, but I manage to smile and say *mmmmm.* They are amused, but I am mortified.

"Tonight you will ave your own room. You are honored guest."

The mattress on the floor of the tiny room looks like heaven to this exhausted body longing to be prone. *Oh! What is this on the wall? A roommate?* My heart pounds—the roach is about three inches long. But I calm myself and decide that from now on, roaches are my friends. I am on a binge diet of *accept everything.* It is the only way.

In the morning several children are on the mattress with me, watching the first white person they have ever seen up close. Everyone is wearing my clothes. My luggage has been ransacked, my shoes put in a household pile of shoes.

Oohhh. Remember yes. Note to self: No personal space or stuff.

The girls giggle as they wrap me in a colorful African cloth. Then a morning meal of . . . nothing, because it is Ramadan and I have slept through the pre–5 a.m. meal I didn't know about.

"Come Diáne, for your hair. It's traditional."

Seven hours later I emerge from the hair dresser with a head full of long, tiny cornrows—and what feels like a facelift from the excruciating hair pulling involved. But with my new African-style braids and attire, I am transformed.

In the street, groups of woman and girls sit in shaded areas under trees, braiding hair, talking, resting. Children collect mangos fallen from nearby trees and fetch well water for the elders. Young men gather in small groups with books and discuss current events. Those lucky enough to attend school sit in structures made from matted straw joined together to make walls, with cardboard and tin sheets as their roofs. Slabs of wood are used as makeshift desks; sheets of dirty cardboard or bits of brown paper serve as blackboards.

The pads of paper and boxes of pencils I brought here have disappeared overnight and I am happy they will be put to such good use. I think of everything my own children have that would be considered a luxury here. How will I raise them to be grateful for the gift of where they were born and all they have.? I miss my kids and wish they could be here to witness such another way of life. But they are too little and too far away. I wonder if they miss me too. I send little gifts for them in hopes they will not forget me.

Most men, women, and children are adorned with numerous *gris-gris*: shells, beads, and leather wound around their arms, legs, waists, and necks for protection. If there is an exam to pass, a husband to attract, an illness, or a wish, a *marabou* is consulted. For a few francs this clairvoyant mystic will sit with you to perceive your energy and divine your problems and your destiny. He will tell you for whom and when to perform certain charitable acts. He may tell you to sacrifice a rooster, buy kola nuts, donate money, wear a certain item, or eat a special food. Then he will go into retreat for several days to perform his magic, after which he will present you with instructions on paper immersed in holy water and charms. He receives an advance on his price and when the magic is complete, the balance of payment. Such a man has given me my *gris-gris*, a tiny conch shell attached to the end of a short braid that falls right over my third eye. This will be my protection for the duration of my journey here.

I love it here despite being totally disoriented as the only white person amid the entire area. I am self-conscious but also feel special and a welcome distraction from the ordinary. to those around me. Two mornings after my arrival a small, shy girl fetches me.

"*We go for special honor.*" Her assignment is to help orient me for the next few days. On the bus I cannot avoid noticing the amusement my presence attracts as I sit squished between several very large women; goats, chickens, children, and men hang out the windows. I pretend it is perfectly normal for me to be the only white person on the bus dressed in African clothing and wearing cornrows. Everyone is limp with sweltering heat but there will be no food or drink until evening, as is the tradition during Ramadan. We fast between 5 a.m. and 8 p.m. There is no sneaking food and we abstain even from water, inhumane as it seems in this heat.

It is deeply humbling to be with small children who are much braver than me about hunger. They mouth prayers, while in my mind I complain and feel ashamed. Pulling out their straw mats just anywhere, people kneel for afternoon prayer. Everything else comes to a stop, even traffic. It seems as natural as washing, walking, or talking. I think about how bored and tense it was sitting on my mother's lap trying to be still through Sunday church. The display of spirituality here seems beautiful, relevant and joyful to me. I am in awe.

Flies, dirt, and children are everywhere. No one seems to mind. Anyone who sees me calls out "*Touba, touba*" (white girl), followed by an exchange of greeting: "*Salamalecoumb. Bonjour, ca va?*" (Peace be unto you. Hello, How is going?) They inquire of each other about the family, the house, the animals. This is repeated ceremonially many times a day, with each encounter. In this totally foreign country I feel more seen and valued then in my own.

Finally arriving at our destination, the girl and I are greeted by tall men looking like sentinels in bloodstained floor-length robes standing amid swarms of flies. The stench is powerful as the procession of men approach me, proffering the carcass of some dead animal in his extended arms. It is my job to choose which we will feast upon at my welcoming celebration. The air is thick. I am sticky from heat, dizzy from hunger, and nauseated by the smell of dead animals. I am trying to be brave and grateful. Trying to keep my *yes* promise, but all this blood and stench. It's too much, too much. My lights go out.

When I come to, I find myself on the bus heading back to the compound. All I can think about is being drenched in a long, warm shower to cleanse and soothe me of this hot, sticky, nauseating day. Upon my arrival my African host proudly points to an open corner of the courtyard used for bathing and offers me a small bucket of cold water. My ration for the day. *Whaaaat? How am I supposed to get clean with only a bucket of water?* Making do becomes my mantra during the next few months. Every moment seems an opportunity to practice that.

Ousmane, age fifteen, is assigned to me to help with my travels. He, like many young boys here is idle with no job or schooling. They just hang around languidly is small groups. His assistance is offered by my Senegalese family who want to make sure I am safe when I leave them for other areas. I will pay for his transport on the hot and overly packed bus- and for food. Where he sleeps at night, nobody knows but during the day he is by my side making sure no one takes advantage of me- the Touba, as we go along so far from Amherst, so far from my babies and loved ones, so far from France. As I observe babies tied their mothers back in a piece of cloth I yearn to hold my own children but keep pushing away a sense of guilt as I inhale all the gifts of the moment I am now in. I know they are well cared for and that has to be enough.

The bus stops after hours on bumpy, dusty roads. We get off in a small village of round thatched huts. Some of the huts are on stilts with ladders reaching up to the opening. These are so at night the children are out of reach of wild animals that may pass through. Ousmane and I walk to a compound with three small houses and a large cooking area in its center. This is the home of some of Ousmane's distant relatives who know we are coming- *But how?* There are no phones, no mailboxes, no stores around. Three beautiful women in colorful booboos walk towards us surrounded by twenty five children. Their children by one man, the patriarch, the husband, the daddy who grows mangos for a living. It is a village unto itself. I have brought gifts. Balloons, face paint and pencils. The children jump in glee immediately clapping, drumming and dancing a welcome for us. Great wooden urns for pounding grain are in the yard ready to be used for the evening meal. The women begin a song to work by and let us know we should get settled. By now I am used to sharing a mattress with children so I am not surprised when there is no bed for me. By the time we are finished with dinner and washing, I will be so tired I could sleep standing up. One more lesson in acceptance and adaptation. A glorious awakening continues.

When I return stateside – brown skin and braided I wonder how my children will react. Michael just looks at me silently when I go to fetch him from day care. Slowly he walks over, sits on my knees and places his head on my shoulder. He does not utter a sound but I can tell the recognition is profound. Maybe he thought he lost me forever. My heart explodes. I am home.

African Days.

Questions:

- Have you ever been completely disoriented in a place that was light years away from your comfort zone?
- Please describe the place and how you felt there.
- How did you handle it and what did you learn from the experience?

20

India—Excerpts

Here is how you drive a scooter in India (specifically, in Mysore). First you find a scooter you like and can pay for. You just jump on it and ride in any direction you like. You ride like this:

In the street, which might be paved and might not, there are many things to negotiate: dogs, cows, people walking, lots of other scooters, busses. So you just *go*, and when you encounter one of those objects, you beep like crazy and then zoom around it. You make sure to toot the horn a lot, like every forty seconds or so. Any person or vehicle will hear the horn and let you pass. If none is present, you toot anyway just to keep in practice.

Here is the best thing about scooter driving: no one needs any kind of license to do it. You just get on and go. Another good thing is how many people can fit on one scooter: lots. Little kids stand just in front of the driver, holding onto the handle bars. Even toddlers do this. Next comes the driver, and then one or two people squished onto the back seat. The back seat people can hold on to babies. And another good thing: no one wears a helmet, so that saves a big expense.

When you cross the street while walking, that's different. You have to go slowly because … oh, I forgot to mention the road rules for drivers—cars, bikes, scooters, and the rest: you can drive on any side of the road, and in any direction, and if someone approaches you beep and swerve, beep and swerve. Which makes it a bit tricky to walk across the road. The dogs and cows don't seem too pleased with this system, and they usually just sit there amid the swerving, but vehicles won't swerve to avoid *people*, so you have to stay out of their way. But that's no problem; you can always tell they're coming because of the tooting. And all this is to negotiate each morning while going from my apartment to the yoga school where I am conducting sound healing workshops for yoga students and learning breathing skills from the owner.

• • •

Twenty times into the left nostril and out the right. Then twenty times into the right and out the left. Hold the breath for a moment after each inhale and exhale. Then watch the in-between breaths. This is how I learn pranayama breathing. At 6 am in the morning just after a yoga class. Oh my God. This place, these things burrow so deeply into my soul. I yearn to know how to bring this feeling back to my own family so they can share it too.

• • •

Close eyes. Index fingers on the eyebrows, fire and water fingers on the eyes, pinky closing the mouth, thumb in the ears ... to hear the sounds of your nervous system.

• • •

Christmas. My first time away from my kids. They are older now but maybe they will miss having me there. I wish they were here but another part of me rejoices in being on my own. Even with no early-morning class, it is hard to stay in bed past 7:30. Even then it is after a morning meditation, practicing some of the pranayama breathing from last week's class. It's unusually quiet this morning, but the sun's rays make their way through the striped orange curtains on my windows. Still, there has to be a special marking of this day ... a celebration. It comes in the form of a cup of tea and a book in bed. In this case, the book is a study of the female brain, and so far I am unimpressed with the writing. The author seems to have put together a work that supports what is already obvious about women's special gifts: women are better at communication, emotions, relationships, language, and so on. No new territory here. So, Sunday morning plans change, and I decide to head to the school to send off a few Merry Christmas emails, then shop for veggies to make a ratatouille for tonight. Maybe I can find some sheets of paper to make wall graffiti in the living room with the housemates Karina and Marc.

As I head out I am surprised to see that Karina is still home; she was supposed to do something with Marc. But no matter—we decide to create a breakfast feast and take it to the roof. Out we go together in search of melons, papayas, flower garlands, and fresh veggies. We find a vendor selling banana leaves and he gifts us with six of them to serve as plates. There is so much generosity from those who have so little. It is humbling. On the roof with its magical view of the town, we set up a colorful cloth; the orange, yellow, and white flower garlands; and the banana leaf plates. Marc is duly impressed when he gets home, and we three officially open our Christmas day with a magnificent feast overlooking Mysore. Heads bowed, hands in prayer position, we each in our own way give thanks for a blessed day, our special company together. Then we devour the food. This, this is sacred. This moment, this day, this being here today giving thanks. I am so happy.

In the afternoon a rickshaw takes me to the pool, and I am determined to see some of the town. Not sure where the pool is, and hoping the driver knows, I insist on the meter, not a negotiated price. The ride takes me farther into town than I have ever been. My nervousness is replaced by the sheer joy of traveling through time and space in this surrey-like vehicle, swerving in and out through the streets. Forty rupees later we arrive at the Reggis Hotel—a majestic palace worlds from how I have been living. It seems like another country: spacious, sparkling clean, regal. Down the steps is the large oval infinity pool. Groups of American sunbathers and European yoga people are sprawled on lounge chairs. The band is playing an assortment of horrible wedding music–type songs. It's hard to bear, but I am determined to make good use of the 250 rupees I've spent to get in here.

The sun is burning but the water is cold. Did I come to India to be in a ritzy hotel among a bunch of other white people slathering sunblock all over themselves? Part of me wants to escape, but I convince myself it's okay to be in this privileged environment for a while before heading back to the hood.

Okay, then. That lounge chair looks fine to me. It's odd, though, to feel out of place among my own kind. What's up with that?

• • •

Tonight, India stole my computer. It was a lovely outing at Akil's house, a huge four-story place with a roof overlooking a calm part of town and hundreds of palm trees. His singing bowl room was a high-ceilinged room containing an altar surrounded by candles. I lay on a platform while he created a series of triads around me to release Kundalini energy. Then he placed a flower on my forehead and a droplet of water.

It was a long rickshaw ride home past the palace. When I arrived back in my room it was obvious that my computer was gone. The shock was losing all my India photos and writings. Plus the invaded privacy. Now I had to hassle with making a police report and an insurance claim. Oddly, though, I felt calm—just sad and curious. How did they get in?

· · ·

It's early morning on the last day in Mysore after a peaceful night's sleep. There are the sounds of the neighbors' pots and pans clanking, monkeys scampering on the wall outside, birds chirping good morning to one another, and the start of the ever present hooting and tooting of bikes, scooters, and cars horns. There is a cup of Tulsi tea beside my bed sweetened with jaggery and a drop of milk. A stream of Mysore incense fills the room. The walls are bare, stripped now of the one small painting gifted to me by Akil, one of my students and fellow sound healer.. A twenty-five-hour journey lies ahead. This month has been a voluptuous gift, dense with rich experiences and sacred moments. As I head back toward the land of plenty, my heart already longs for the simplicity of the life I have found here. It hasn't been enough time. I haven't delved deeply enough into the part of myself where there is nothing to do and nowhere to go. Still, here my soul and spirit feel so much more settled among a community where the focus is on peace, yoga, loving acceptance, and a sense of connection with the vendors, the children, and even the dogs …

Questions:

- Where have you found a sense of deep peace in a surprising context?
- What was that like?
- What do you do to reclaim that feeling when challenges present themselves?

21

CRAIG

We sit in the field, the shaman and I. He gives me some weed and begins to strum his guitar. Not a song, or even a melody, but a series of sounds that send me into a trance, afloat on a river of wandering notes. In that trance-like state I suddenly hear my mother's voice, sharp and condescending, with her strong French accent. It is an abrupt departure from the melodic interlude. She is talking to my little brother, who is, in my mind's eye, curled up in my arms. I imagine myself to be about ten.

"Don't talk to him like he is a dog, Maman."

Maman detested animals. "Move, dog," she would say if one crossed her path. Like it didn't deserve to live. And she used that same cutting voice with my brother because he was a little different, and she didn't know how to handle him. I hated that voice and tried to protect him from it. But being a small child myself and holding him in my arms, I could feel his spirit dying. He railed against the demise of his spirit in the only way he knew how. And my mother couldn't deal with it.

And then I understand. Amid the soft chords of the shaman's guitar and the effects of the weed, I finally know something. The dark force that greets me each morning; the strong pull that tries to ensnare me like a harbinger of death; the looming darkness within my body from my solar plexus down the left side of my torso, pulling the life out of me; the waves of deep, restless anxiety trying to drag me into the vortex of no return. I finally know what it is. *Guilt.* Guilt because I could not save my little brother. That feeling like thick tar every single morning for years.

So I've had to jump out of bed and move. *Do something, do something, do something*—anything to shake off the feeling of being pulled into death myself. Jump up, make bed, brush teeth, move, move, move. Only then can I come back into myself and start my day.

Now I recognize the dark energy that has presented itself each morning for what it is, and with the help of some medicinal herbs and the shaman's hypnotic music, I can finally let it go—you cannot release what you don't own. It has taken decades for me to own my guilt over being helpless to save my brother. I, his big sister, felt his life force fighting for itself when we were just children. I saw my mother sabotaging his spirit but did not yet have the tools to protect him. I was only a little girl, and she was my mother too.

Craig was a taxing child. He was also short, and he seemed to need to assert himself through his actions rather than his size. At any moment, if something upset him, he might throw utensils across the dinner table at us or wipe out an entire shelf at the supermarket with his arm. His ability to tease relentlessly could drive my older brother, John, to tears. Every week Craig stole paper route money from John and watched silently as my father berated him for being so stupid as to lose money. But Craig was also funny, sweet, and generous. He was smart and loveable. There was no telling which part of him would show up in any situation. Doctors had no name for what he had going on and certainly no effective treatment or advice at that time besides *"He'll grow out of it."*

And he did. When as a teenager he finally grew in stature, his erratic tendencies were replaced by a sweet docility, though he never lost his sense of humor as the clown of any party. He was very attached to maman with a strong need to impress her, which was impossible since her unspoken expectations could never be met.

He started smoking weed in high school. Any drug coupled with a delicate disposition is not a good combination. During his first year at college he took his girlfriend to Jamaica on school break. When they were boarding the plane home, he suddenly left her and returned instead to their rental unit to swallow barbiturates, his first attempted suicide. The landlady discovered him in time to rush him to the hospital.

Over the course of the next few years there were several more attempts. He spent time in an institution from which he was dismissed for smuggling in drugs. When my parents finally divorced, Dad took charge and hired a full-time housekeeper to keep an eye on him during the day. Craig seemed to slowly regain control and be on the way to a better life. Then, just a few days prior to his twenty-first birthday, he was found in a parking lot where he had asphyxiated himself in the housekeeper's car, stolen when she went to bed.

During that time I was living in Paris with Yuma. He walked into our little kitchenette where I was cutting Swiss chard for the evening meal and solemnly announced, *"Well, he did it. Your father called and wanted me to tell you."* Then he just stood there staring at me.

What in hell is he talking about? Then the thunderbolt hit. All the liquid in my body seemed to be sucked out as I dropped, in slow motion, to the floor. *Oh, God. Oh, God.* My sweet little brother. *Why, why , why did you do that? Could I have helped you somehow? You left me, all of us. I can't stand it.* I could feel my body but could not move it. I could hear the sound of my own breath as if I were in an incubator. It was as though there was nothing but breath. If its sound ceased, I would disappear.

Without my really knowing it, breath had always saved me., even before learning Pranayama in India. Long, deep breaths, in through the nose and out through the mouth, extending the exhalations to calm me. Rapid breathing to energize me and keep me from falling asleep at the wheel during long night drives. The breathing that held me together after my brother's death, the sensation of becoming breath. Again and again, breath has come to my rescue. Holding myself, rocking back and forth at the fireplace holding Thomas with Yuma's note in my hand—in inconceivable despair, breath was there to cradle me.

That time at midnight when I landed at the Boston airport carrying my infant son and all my possessions and my sister did not come to meet me, breath calmed me down, held me together, and guided me to my destination. Twice, helping thwart the pain of childbirth, breath, quick and strong, was my anchor to reality. *Keep breathing. Keep breathing.* The focus on the breath rather than the pain incited determination, the survival instinct, and tremendous power. The thought, the reminder that with breath, intentional and focused, come peace, tranquility, and a return to the present moment. At first, it was just instinctive; I didn't yet regard it as a most vital tool. Later, older, I realized the power and potency of breath and its role in personal transformation.

There are so many things that live within us at the same time: love/hate, understanding/judgment, joy/pain. Poet Kahlil Gibran wrote, *"Your pain is the breaking of the shell that encloses your understanding."* We wrestle with conflicting emotions while attempting to find balance. The conflict can manifest into physical ailments that access every aspect of our lives—or even cause death.

In the end, we have to endure the condition of our life. Or not.

For many years I thought that Craig took his life so I didn't have to take mine—a sacrifice to purge the toxicity in our family. I now know that his death had nothing to do with me, for we are all fully responsible for our choices. It may take years, but my path is to be kind to myself and others, to choose compassion over judgment and joy over pain. This is an ongoing path that offers copious occasions to fail. Multiple bruises are a testimony to that. The Buddhist belief that the universe is compassionate does not mean that it is easy. It means that we will make the same mistakes over and over again until the lesson is learned. We will be presented with obstacles that can catapult us into learned toxic behaviors and attitudes until we become bigger and better at being human. It can take a lifetime, and along the way we have to figure out what is important, what isn't, when to stand up and when to be quiet, what feels authentic and what doesn't, what is power and what is control. Life is a never-ending obstacle course with no real end in sight. I have learned that pain is a pathway to understanding. It takes many times around the block to get that. My brother chose an end when still just a child.

Craig

Questions:

- What is your relationship with death?
- What are your fears, if any about your own or other people's death
- How do your spiritual beliefs influence your attitude to death?
- Have you experienced the suicide of a close friend or relative?
- What did you learn from that?

22

MARLENE

The Microbiology of Cancer is my favorite course in 1980 when I return to the US from Europe. The professor is a slight, olive-skinned Jewish man of undeterminable age who eats a macrobiotic diet. He presents lectures on cancer from a variety of perspectives by showing us repulsive films of gory surgeries on smoke-damaged lungs, or of cancer patients sharing their journeys with heart-wrenching authenticity. I have no idea that in the future I will be doing sound healing treatments for cancer patients.

My good friend and fellow student Marlene is dying of cancer herself. Once again I am working through a loved ones journey that can lead to sudden death. I am witnessing courage up close and my heart longs to be able to make a difference in her life. We go to classes together and take long walks. She shares with me her ideas about how she is going to get past the pain, her decisions about her treatment, and her confusion about what to do with her huge teepee. Most of the time I am at a loss at how to help her but being a witness to her pain seems to help her. During one lecture she suddenly turns to me: *"My whole right arm just went numb. I can't feel anything."* With that she transfers her pen from right to left hand and announces that she will now become a lefty.

That is how Marlene goes through her ordeal. Nothing seems to get her down except the constant and progressing pain. After an initial trial of chemotherapy and the ensuing hair loss, she ditches traditional treatments. I am watching and learning how to die with grace and courage. It enrages me that she, so beautiful and young has to endure this. Where is God? Where is fairness? Prior to her leaving to work on a pot farm in Hawaii so she can minimize her pain with weed, we have hours of raucous fun choosing scarves and fashioning them into crazy headpieces for her to wear. My heart breaks when she leaves knowing I will probably never see her again.

· · ·

We kept in touch until she could no longer write. She moved back in with her parents to transition in peace. Her mom sent me a letter Marlene had dictated just before she passed. It simply said how much fun she had enjoyed during her life, and she thanked us, her friends, for our love. She didn't want any of us to be sad and expressed only gratitude for what she'd had.

I wonder at how she was able to stay so focused on what was working for her, on her joy, all the while enduring such turbulence. *Could I do that?* She never asked, "Why me?" or complained about her condition. Instead she considered what would be the best choice in each situation that presented itself on her journey, as a witness rather than a victim of her circumstance. And she left her teepee to me.

Questions:

- Who do you know that taught you strength and courage by how they navigated their life challenges?
- How did you integrate that into your life?

23

FIRE!

"Holy shit! No! I can't believe this!"

Everyone is standing around, shifting uncomfortably from one foot to the other. A few people are banging on doors, but I just stand motionless. Flames explode from the rooftops like the finale of a fireworks display. There is a massive amount of smoke, and the fire is being sucked through the roof vents, jumping from one apartment to the next.

At 8:30 a.m. my boys, just four and nine, are starting their day at school. Upon their return their world will have changed. It is all gone. Everything we own.

Well there goes my past, all the possessions, all the shit. Time to create new karma.

My brain is thinking this but my body isn't moving. Then a tentative tap on my shoulder. A hand offering me a coupon. It's the Red Cross, a cheery Red Crosser with a coupon for one towel, two sheets, one blanket, one change of clothes for each of us. Oh, and another coupon for one dinner and lodging tonight. Somebody says, "*Thanks so much. That's very kind.*" It may be me. It sounds like my voice but if my mouth has moved, I'm not aware of it.

There is a place in Amherst that stocks expired cans of food, old donated clothing, and furniture, mostly broken: the Survival Center. All the winos and homeless people go there. That's where we get a few mangy mattresses.

A couple of units in the complex are slated for renovation. One of them had previously housed students and needed an upgrade. Badly. Broken pipes, peeling paint, holes in the wall, old vomit on the carpet. Animal House: we are put in there. There is a class action suit by the eight of us who lost our homes. The complex management is responsible. We will get a settlement, a small one that will take months to receive. We are disoriented and keep searching for things until we remember they're gone. We wear the same clothing for days, exist on oodles of noodles for weeks, and are often in a daze.

But we put our scrounged-up mattresses on the threadbare carpet, survive on donations and the Survival Center, and call our new place home. Little by little, it becomes that too.

After a while, suddenly the notion of having "lost everything" seems bogus. It's been traumatic and inconvenient, for sure, but what we've lost is just stuff and

THE GIFT IN THE WOUND

what we've found is a closer connection to one another, a strengthening of character, resourcefulness, and resolve. The boys seem to take on the challenge as a badge of honor, and they too notice the display of human kindness afforded us by friends and family. It is humbling. Our sense of gratitude for the smallest things expands our hearts and our compassion for others. We have been challenged but we have discovered that we are not our stuff, for we are each far bigger than our possessions. In the loss of our home, the strength of the human spirit and a closer encounter with our essence emerge as the greatest of gifts.

Questions:

- What situation helped you to focus on what is really most important in your life?
- Can you remember a time where you had to let go completely and accept the unacceptable?
- What was that situation?
- In what way did that help you in your life?

24

CUBA, 1988

Raucous cheering arises from the throngs of joyous employees standing in the entranceway of the "campo." It is an enthusiastic, heartwarming welcome as we step off the bus. The twenty Venceremos Brigade individuals who have circumvented restrictions and made their way to Cuba when it is forbidden are exhibiting their unwavering support for us. I cannot believe we did this. Cannot believe I am here. Every pore in my body is vibrating from the exhilaration of having pulled this off and at the same time feel deeply humbled by the reception from a people toward whom our country, the US, has been so ugly.

In a further act of rebellion, shoving aside recurring waves of fear, I present my passport to be stamped upon arrival, rather than having just a piece of paper stamped that can later be removed so customs agents won't know of my trip to Cuba. After months of study and preparation, we all flew to Canada first and then boarded another flight to Havana. Upon ensuing trips in and out of the US, I will be greeted by customs officials saying, "We know where you have been." But their threatening attitude is wasted on me. I just feel empowered by having pulled it off.

Venceremos Brigade is a group dedicated to promoting friendship and understanding between the US and Cuba. We are there to learn about Cuban culture and help where possible. We cannot spend US dollars here, so we are fully hosted and given a symbolic two pesos each. Housing is simple dorm-style cabins with a cafeteria, group bathrooms, and a facility for washing clothing. Meals are mostly rice, beans, eggs, fruit, and occasionally chicken and ice cream. I deeply love the simplicity of it all and the sense of connection to all members of the group. This is what opens my heart.

"*Buenos dias, amigos y amigas. Es un hermosa dia*" is blasted over a loudspeaker at 6 a.m. every morning after we've had only a few hours of sleep. Cubans really know how to party. Every night guitars and percussion suddenly appear in the campo, and a frenzy of mambo and rhumba dancing ensues into all hours of the night. The dance is so sexy it is impossible not to fall in love with everyone. So at 6 a.m., groggy but happy, we grab a quick breakfast and jump into the backs of dilapidated trucks to pick oranges in the heat of a nearby orchard. The oranges are sold at local markets and help fund the activities at the campo. Again this sense of purposefulness rises within me. The feeling of love within me expands when I can be of service.

Each day, after a box lunch under a shaded citrus tree and a short siesta, we are taken on an outing to visit prisons, senior centers, institutions for mental illness, and special schools. Evenings, prior to the dance parties, we participate in lectures by invited guests that delve into issues confronting the country such as the gay rights, building community, support for musicians and farmers, and the fate of exiled political prisoners. Lecturers seem to speak freely and are happy to share their perspectives with Americans. Nothing seems like all the negative American propaganda I have heard all my life about Cuba. Why oh why do politics dismiss the beauty and humanity of people in different countries? I hate meeting fantastic people and knowing that they are being misrepresented because of politics. What can I do to change the perception about Cuba?

The women's prison offers a hair and nail salon where inmates may go to boost their sense of self-esteem. There is a specially decorated room set aside for inmates to see their families, as well as some small private rooms for intimate encounters with spouses. Women are rehabilitated rather than just punished. Educational opportunities are part of their daily routine, as is manufacturing products that are needed in the outside world such as license plates for cars. The incarcerated women seem as curious and happy to meet us as we are to meet them. If they are being forced to act or say certain things in order to make a good impression on us, it would be a surprise, because it all certainly feels authentic. I am beyond grateful for this opportunity to be invited into another culture, another way of seeing the world. How did I get so lucky?

Walking around the city feels like being in a time bubble from the 1950s, with old cars and beautiful architecture everywhere. Cubans have figured out how to jury-rig the parts they can't get from the US because of the American embargo. Resourceful! Truly a testimony to "challenge is the mother of invention."

An ancient-looking woman is strikingly beautiful: snow white hair, large brown eyes, softly wrinkled, well-tanned skin. Her arms are lifted toward the sky, and her head is thrown back as she laughs joyously to the music. She is part of the senior center where a group of very old citizens are doing their fitness routine outdoors. They seem happy and healthy, and are having fun. Eager to engage with me, several recount how they came to this center in a wheelchair unable to walk but now feel so much more independent, with a higher quality of life. Once a week children arrive, and the elderly read to them, acting as gentle grandparents to the kids. Over and over again, seniors say, "We were so repressed under Batista. Fidel Castro changed everything and gave us our lives back. Everyone gets food now due to rationing programs, and fitness classes outdoors make us healthy. We love it here."

I am continually reminded how important it is to question what we read and hear about a place. Doing my own research provides me with a completely different perspective from what I have been taught about Cuba. I wonder how I can impress the importance of questioning upon my own children to help them be more conscious humans.

Friday is a special day for schoolchildren. Mornings find them in the fields learning to grow food. Afternoons are dedicated to attending a vocational school offering a choice of apprenticeships in a huge range of vocations, from gymnastics to glass blowing to postal or electrical work to engineering. Each apprenticeship is for a year, and students may stay with the same field or change it each year. By the time the kids graduate, they have a visceral understanding of their fields of interest and can better choose what to focus on in college. Brilliant, but seen as "forced labor" in the US. I think of all the people I know who spent thousands on collage but never knew what they wanted to do when they got out. I was so fortunate to travel with my mother as a child and be gifted with a broader perspective of the world.

Some afternoons I was dropped off in the center of Havana to stroll around and talk to people which was a surprise, as I expected to be closely watched and forbidden to roam freely. This put me in touch with a number of people who were angry: musicians who were not allowed to tour outside Cuba or get the instruments of their choice, and some who had toured and felt restricted after their return. The gay community was exceptionally repressed and punished—not so different from many other parts of the world, including the US. But in general people seemed happy and protective of their country. The idea of "each man for himself" over "the good for all" seemed reprehensible to them. Community support always trumped individual advancement.

Upon my return to the US, radio stations reached out for interviews. "Stop trying to put words in my mouth," I told them. "I only have positive and inspiring things to say about my visit. It's a beautiful country, and the people are great, so if you are looking for reports of repressive Communist agendas and a miserable, starving population, you will not get that from me."

It was in the context of one of the evening lectures in Cuba that I met Saths Cooper, who had spent nine years locked away, five and a half of them (1977–82) in the same cell block as Nelson Mandela at the Robben Island prison off the coast of Cape Town. When we met in Havana, he was delivering speeches about imprisonment during apartheid.

Saths eventually landed in Boston, where I received an invitation to attend the celebration of his birth. The room was pregnant with people, many of them white (including myself), discussing things that mattered.

"Saths, how is it possible for you to be in a room with so many white people when it is whites who imprisoned you for so many years. Aren't you angry at them? At us?" I asked.

Saths took me into another room where we could talk privately. He sat me down and explained something that left an indelible mark on my soul. He told me that in prison, his cell was right near the children's cells. Lots of kids were scooped up and thrown in jail when the police came for their parents. They were hungry, and beaten, even sodomized. And they cried. They screamed and wailed. He could hear them perfectly, but there was nothing he could do. He felt so bad. So, so bad. But when you are locked up, nobody cares how you feel. If you're hungry, or sick, if you are suffering or angry. No one cares. No one will do anything to help you. He could not change anything outside himself. The only thing that made sense, that made it possible for him to survive, that helped him feel better, was to cultivate love. Just love. When he felt the emotion of love, he could feel something good. So he does not hate; he does what he can to change a bad situation. But he chooses to love.

Saths, who is now a doctor of psychology, gave me a teaching that day about compassion that remains the most impressive of my life. I am not sure I could do what he did if that situation presented itself in my life. It is so easy to go into anger, hate, and blame. But in the most horrific and dire circumstances, he chose love. So that must be my ultimate destination, always.

Tibetan Buddhism teaches us not to blindly accept what we are told about anything. The journey to Cuba was a stellar example of the need to check things out for myself, something I have tried to do all my life.

Questions:

- Think about a time when you were surprised by having a totally different experience of a place or person from what you have been told to expect.
- What did you learn from that?

- In what way might you shift your emotions about a traumatic event from negative to empowering?
- What do you have to believe in order to do that?
- Where the gift in that experience?

25

ANA

Everyone has one best friend. Or should. Even if it is a little turtle or a grasshopper or a puppy or a girlfriend. I met mine in 1981. She was sitting on the floor in the high school gym in Amherst where we were both taking our toddlers for karate lessons. I, recently returned from living in France; she, a dark brunette, café au lait–skinned Costa Rican woman. Possibly the most beautiful I had ever seen. When I walked into the room she turned and smiled. My heart flipped; there was no hesitation on my part. I just walked over and sat down next to her. Somehow, we were already friends.

We fit one another; she could practice her French with me, and I had an international friend; she was like the sister of my dreams. True family comes in many forms, as blessings do. We learn through the family we were born into but often feel loved by people outside that circle. Over the years, Ana and I have been there for one another in every way: child rearing, higher education, boyfriends to husbands to ex-husbands, empty nests, menopause, all the joys and the tears.

When I was dirt poor and on welfare, she always found little jobs for me to do at her house that she could pay me for—build a garden, paint the walls. She certainly had to hire someone to redo the grout between the tiles in the kitchen after I got through doing that job, but she never mentioned it. A few months after the fire that destroyed my home, once I had settled my family, she took me on a two-week trip to Mexico so I could release all the stress. Dancing in elegant halls, listening to romantic music, licking Mexican ice pops, eating tostadas, and exploring the beach scene in Puerto Escondido, Oaxaca, nourished my beaten-down spirit.

Ana saved me.

No matter where I am in my life, just knowing she's there is grounding enough. It helps me feel safe. We nurture the joy of our sisterhood in every way possible: spontaneous road trips, little messages, phone calls.

We don't need many friends—but we do need a best friend to share life's intimacies with. A friend like that is the glue that holds all the different parts of a life together. A lifeline.

Ana

Questions:

- Who is your best friend? Why?
- What part of you shows up when you are with them?
- What is the difference between this friend and others?

26

SALSA! SUNDAY NIGHT. TEN O'CLOCK.

Ten p.m.? Are you crazy? Who goes out at 10 p.m. on a Sunday? I do. I leave my sleeping children. The tenant is downstairs in case of need.

The Royal China restaurant has a large dance floor, a good sound system, and a colorful laser light ball. That's where I head, so looking forward to warm, gyrating bodies, the scent of a hundred colognes, and everyone dressed to the nines. There's a feeling about the dance: a rush that fills my body with a sense of purpose and freedom, like reaching deep into myself for my true identity. My swirling, whirling, fully expressive self.

I have a miniskirt for the occasion. It's always the same one but I don't think anyone knows or cares. I am barely making the mortgage payments, so springing for a new skirt is not going to happen. But women who wear skirts rather than slacks get invited to dance more, and I just want to dance.

The room is packed with bodies. Puerto Ricans, Cubanos, Africans, Filipinos, and Jamaicans. Everyone is happy. One of only a few white girls there, I boldly venture onto the dance floor, stepping to the beat of the *wahwahco*. It feels good to know eyes are watching me—apparently some white girls have moves. Soon enough a curious bystander approaches and we *merengue*.

It's a lifeline: moving, swaying, following my partner's lead exactly, hips cemented together, his arm strong against my back. We move as one. Every part of me releasing completely into rapid-fire twirls. One, two, three, then six in a row, round and round, then whipped back into his arms and all in perfect time. People are watching. Everything disappears except This Moment, when I am weightless and flying this way and that. Clearly in the dance, spirit looms larger than body.

Each time the music ends, I stagger off the floor to stand against the wall, wipe my brow, and catch my breath and the eye of the next young man making his way toward me. It's like this from 10 until midnight every Sunday, dance after dance. Here I relinquish the stress, the disappointments, the challenges and fears of my life, the isolation and unending struggle of single parenting.

In the sacred moments I spend here, I am rejuvenated with resolve, enthusiasm, and even a sense of self-love in recognition of something I can do so well. I know that my excitement will be met each Sunday by those looking forward to their time with me too. And that nourishes the empty place within me that needs to be seen and touched and loved. At least for another week.

Questions:

- Do you have a passion that helps you deal with life's challenges?
- What is it?
- How do you feel when engaged with that passion?
- How much time and energy do you give to your passion?

27

ROTARY

It feels odd standing there. I have a "not really me" sensation wearing my grown-up outfit: black pumps, gray rayon suit, just the right piece of jewelry—a red accent around the neck.

There is some clinking as forks pick up the last morsels of chicken cacciatore before waitresses slink in quietly (as they've been instructed) to exchange lunch plates for small porcelain cups of coffee and little squares of vanilla crumb cake.

It is time, and all faces turn expectantly toward me. Newspaper people are poised at the ready to get that perfect picture, one of those caught-mid-sentence-with-finger-pointing-energetically-up-and-head-cocked shots.

That would be me—Action Woman. That's why I've been hired. To give the town a boost, an infusion of *je ne sais quoi*, something to send the old coots still running the place out on their asses and bring in new blood, new ideas. Make the town thrive again.

And now is my moment to tell them how it is to be done. All the doctors, the attorneys, the mayor and staff, the prominent business folk—all here waiting expectantly for my wisdom. Something to applaud, to grin and bob heads over, sure now that they've picked the right woman for the job.

And this is what comes out of my mouth:

"You all know me. For the past twenty years we have passed each other in the street. I have bought items from your shops, sat in your waiting rooms with my sniveling children, and volunteered in your schools. Most of the time I was not noticeable to you. Now, every word I say is printed with my smiling picture beside it. You all want to stop me to shake hands when we cross paths. When you say my name to your friends, it is a big deal now. Every time I do something you want to give me a badge or some kind of honor. Well, I don't need that now. When I did, you just turned away, embarrassed by my need. Every single woman who is raising her children alone needs a badge of recognition and a handshake in the street to let her know somebody cares about the job she is doing. That is the hardest of jobs. Especially if you're on welfare. This is a piece of cake. But none of you shook my hand or even returned a smile when I was in that role.

"*I am the same person now as I was then. Maybe you could all ponder that as you finish your cake.*"

And then I walk out. *What the hell? Oh, my God, who just said that?* Oh, no, *I didn't just do that. Now, right now, I have absolutely got to pee something awful. But Jesus, how can I go back in there? Mortified, I just mortified myself. Good job, Diáne. I'm sure no one will forget your first speech at the Rotary Club as the new director of the Chamber of Commerce.*

And then a bunch of "those people" are running out of the restaurant toward me. *Oh, God, oh, God.* But no . . . they're crying. Suddenly I'm the hub of a massive group embrace. I see stern-faced professionals with tears in their eyes. Thanking me. *They didn't realize. They are so sorry. The best speech they ever heard.*

After that—things just got better.

Rotary

Questions:

- Was there a time in your life when you totally showed up but were also mortified by the effect it had on others? Please describe .

28

CANCER SOCIETY

How exactly am I going to make it through today?
I can't do this anymore. I can't do this anymore. I
can't do this anymore.

This is what I say to myself as I put my face on and
brush my chin-length hair styled to say "executive."

"*The one thing I wasn't looking forward to in this job,*" I
say to the CEO during my job interview at the huge home
office of the Cancer Society in Boston, "*was having to dress
up for the office. I'm so glad to see people dressed in jeans. What
a relief.*"

He pauses, then: *It's dress-down Friday. Every other day
all the regional executive directors have to wear a red jacket
and black skirt.*

Talk about foot in mouth disease. I got the job but should have known better right then and there. The money is good, though, better than the Chamber of Commerce job, and I am sick to death of saying, "*No, we can't afford it*" to my kids. It is another seat-of-my-pants job: I have no idea how to run a huge nonprofit.

Note to self: *Don't ever, ever do something just for the money. It kills the soul. It leaves a hole so deep you feel like the walking dead.*

But a high tolerance for pain keeps me there for two and a half years. I create endless fundraising events, wrestle over budgets, endure long drives to boring meetings in Boston, host volunteer dinners with grace, fight like hell to diversify the white-bread staff, since our new office is in a mainly Hispanic town. I give a lot and learn a lot. Until it is no longer possible.

"*Boys, go find some lawns to mow because I am quitting my job. There will be milk in the fridge but maybe not much more.*"

"*Mooooommmm! No, Mom, c'mon. You can't do this. You're supposed to take care of us.*"

"*Okay, so what do you want, guys—a dead mother or a happy mother? Because that's the choice at this point.*"

They were leaning toward a dead mother, but then logic got the best of them and they got neighborhood jobs, from lawn mowing to selling dope. My darling neighbor kept an eye on them for two days while I went on a retreat at Kripalu to clear my head and figure out the next chapter in my life. It wasn't an easy thing for a single mom to do:

take time to regroup. Leave underage kids at home and worry constantly.

"While I'm gone you boys need to paint the kitchen. It needs to be very, very pale yellow with green cupboards. That should keep you busy and out of trouble. Thomas, you're in charge. Here's the money to get the paint, and Emily will keep an eye on you both. I will call you every day to make sure everything is okay. Please help me make this work. I really need it."

So starts my life as an energy worker. I take weekend classes two and a half hours' drive from my now bright banana yellow kitchen with its greenish floor where the paint accident happened. The extra room upstairs becomes my healing room.

The kids think I've gone mad. Every time Michael walks past the room during a session, his eyes roll in his head and he mumbles, *"Mom, can't you get a real job?"* But it pays the bills and gives me something to do that feels nourishing and authentic. After more than two years in hell, life is finally better. Much better.

Questions:

- When did you abandon something secure for a passion?
- What were your thoughts and motivation?
- How often have you disregarded your deep calling for money?
- What do you need to believe about yourself to change that?

29

NEPAL, 2000

"*Are there a lot more hills like this one?*" I ask, panting and trying to ignore the burning in my thighs and lungs. "*Oh, just little bit more,*" is the guide's response.

Richard and I have embarked upon our first major trip since the inception of our relationship in Amherst. We have been walking for the last six hours in Nepal's luscious, mountainous Langtang Valley with Thomas and Andrew, Richard's son. It was promoted as a three-week excursion, but we don't have that much time so we're doing it in two weeks, which demands a rigorous pace of eight to ten hours of daily trekking.

And there is nothing valley-like about the Langtang Valley. It's often hand over fist, uphill, downhill, uphill, through jungles full of shrieking monkeys, leeches, and snakes—but also glorious waterfalls, stupas, Tibetan flags blowing in the wind, sweet tiny villages, and the majesty of Himalayan mountain vistas.

Heat and debilitating humidity are the norm for the monsoon season. As we ascend through the rainforest to our first stopover, visions of an ice cold drink and a comfortable bed lure us forward. We make a few stops to offer gratitude at a stone stupa atop a precarious ridge overlooking a drop of hundreds of feet, or to have a quick lunch of *dal bhat*, the meal of curried rice, lentils, and potatoes that is prepared three times a day every day for the duration. There are no roads, just barely perceptible paths swarming with tiny bugs. But on this first day we are filled with the naïve vision of what awaits us. This heat, this fatigue, this is just the newness of the first day of hiking with all our gear. *It will surely become easier as we gain strength.* We sing a little Tibetan walking song as we hike, led by our trusty guide, Sanjay, and one Sherpa who carries food. We are well equipped with our high-tech walking sticks, extra-tread Merrell boots, sun-deflecting hats, hiking pants that zip off to create shorts, and breathable rain gear. When it isn't raining, the sun is brutal. The guide and the Sherpa wear flip-flops and thin chinos. For snacks, we munch on nutritious trail mix. They ingest handfuls of dry oats.

When we arrive at our evening destination, we spot a small pond atop the mountainside location where we are to rest for the night. Since our early morning departure we have not seen a single other human, and now we are on a high mountain surrounded by other high mountains in the middle of nowhere. Our reward for the day is warm Cokes transported here over several weeks on the sturdy backs of Sherpas. This is the manner in which all supplies are brought to the lodges along the Langtang Valley—and not just food: wood, generators, refrigerators, solar cells … every, every, everything needed for survival is carried in this way. So there are no complaints when our bed turns out to be a wooden slab with some straw on top under a ramshackle roof.

Every day brings its gifts of wonder, magic, and hell. Maybe we do get stronger, but the mountains get higher, the oxygen gets scarcer, and the rigors of the day mount. When we think our physical limit had been reached and we cannot make one. more. step. our skilled guide moves us along, promising *"Almost there, almost there."* Hours later when we complain, he coyly explains, *"Sorry, sorry, I forgot about big mountain in between."*

Suddenly I am wailing. We have been instructed to tuck our pants inside our socks and wear cloth shields over our boots and the hems of our pants. This to prevent leeches from accessing our legs. Which they do anyway somehow—we discover them at night munching under our socks. *How did they get in there with all our preventative gear?* I am wailing as I discover that here in Nepal, leeches drop out of the trees or jump up from the ground. My meltdown starts while I'm attempting to remove them from my boots with a long stick.

And suddenly, I stop. Stop wailing, stop being afraid. Stop acting like such a girl. Because in a flash it dawns on me that my emotional state is pointless.

We are in the middle of nowhere. Nothing is going to change. No one is coming to save me. Leeches are here to stay and so am I. There is no point in anything save acceptance. I do not have to love it, but I must accept it and soldier on. Which I do. Not only then but for the entire rest of the journey. Almost.

What a miracle to have gotten ourselves to this unbelievable place together. What an amazing gift to spend three weeks with my twenty-year-old son and my lover, trekking, adventuring, and exploring a place I have yearned to know for a lifetime. Here we are and I am miserable. Richard is just not paying enough attention to me. I want to know beyond a shadow of a doubt that I am the priority in his life. He is paying far too much attention to his son and his Tibetan friends. Thomas reminds me that *he* is here with me too—and can't that be enough? We are hiking at 16,000 feet and I am storming around, mad as hell because I haven't been kissed enough or held enough or whatever an insecure woman needs to make herself feel cherished. My amazing son is there with me and I am ignoring that gift. Richard is beyond caring and I am on a fucking outrageous mountaintop in Nepal having a fit and almost, yes, almost missing the whole point of everything.

Down in the valley we arrive at a little hut. It is not unlike other little huts save a few creative adaptations. In these parts, yak dung is collected, dried, and used for many things—usually making fires. Sometimes it is mixed with other materials to make the outer walls of a home. In this case, however, the old man hosting us made a lovely paste out of yak dung and used it as interior plaster. The cots are pushed up against the yak dung walls, and no way am I going to sleep like that. Period. What about acceptance? Not tonight! So I drag the cots to the middle of the room and tuck in for a fretful, smelly night.

In the morning, as if to reward us for making it through the night, we are presented with a gift: one hard-boiled egg each. Apparently our host found a way to preserve some eggs that had been brought up who knows when. We ignore the bits of green on the egg white and hope for the best. The taste is exhilarating after our mono diet of *dal bhat*.

The boys, all of them in my little posse, head out just a few minutes before me, hopping over slimy boulders to cross the ravaging river. A river that if one fell in would certainly lead to immediate death. My short legs would never allow me to hop from one slimy rock to the next. I am terrified, glued to the bank of that river—paralyzed in fear while contemplating my options: cross and suffer a horrible traumatic death, or head back alone on foot for days, probably get lost, and die that way. I just stand there, suspended in unknowing.

And then a guardian angel appears, in the form of my son Thomas. He must have finally noticed my absence and doubled back for me, his only mama. He crosses the river, takes my pack, extends his hand, and smiles. He feels my terror and is gentle with me every time my foot slips and I panic. Then we are on the other side.

Hours later we arrive at a tiny community of just a few stone huts on the side of the mountain. Our hosts include several beautiful large-eyed children with colorful clothing made from what seem to be woven strips of potato sack material; their heart-penetrating smiles shine a brilliant white. On the paths leading to the huts we come upon women in ragged skirts with long braids and wrinkled, deeply tanned faces. Though they look to be ninety years old, they carry on their backs enormous loads of sticks and yak dung for firemaking in long woven baskets and ascend the hill with agility and grace while we slog upward in all our tech gear. *I believe I am morphing into a man. All the feminine aspects of myself have deserted me in order to complete this arduous but astonishing journey.*

Up ahead is one hut with long oversized shelves divided into cubbies containing sheets: our sleeping quarters. It is an ingenious way to fit two rows of hikers, one atop the other, and offers a tiny bit of privacy between sleeping bags. We are ravenous, so having *dal bhat* again for the millionth time is okay. Practically anything tastes good after hiking all day, and we are filled with gratitude knowing that someone had to bring the sacks of food up the mountain on their back.

"*Where is the toilet, please?*" She points to a tiny outhouse on the precipice of the cliff, a wooden structure with a hole in the floor and a bucket of water. Under the floor there is only vast emptiness for hundreds and hundreds of feet. *What holds this structure up?*

Squatting on a cliff with nothing below for what seems to be miles is not conducive to elimination of any kind. Every muscle in the body contracts with the vision of falling through that hole into a great abyss. And yet there is little choice so high in the mountains with no trees to hide behind.

Again, that familiar feeling that our human limits are at their absolute end, the terror of possible imminent death. This is not an everyday sensation, but there are several of these occasions during this glorious, life-altering pilgrim's journey. In such situations the shift in attitude is immediate—like dropping a piece of hot coal. It is the only way to go on without being in constant discomfort.

• • •

Looking back on that time, I wonder why it is still a challenge to let go of belief systems that do not serve. Do we really have to be in a situation we perceive as life threatening to release our sense of limitation? Chaos abounds and always will as we navigate through it. But it seems that we keep needing to learn our lessons over and over again.

In Nepal my emotions flipped from trauma to ecstasy within moments. There I learned lessons to help me navigate humanity: this vast terrain of constant exploration in which I seem to always be a student, tripping along through my life and hopefully getting a little better along the way. I encountered myself capable of holding an expanded perspective of a situation, offering the benefit of the doubt to others, countered by a small self mistaking itself for the center of the universe, taking everything personally and forgetting that at any given moment whatever is happening, however tragic or ecstatic, is still just a blip on the screen.

And so it was that on a high mountain in Nepal, out of the blue at 17,000 feet, from a reservoir of inner wisdom I did not know was there, looking out at the vast canopy of peaks below me, I made an announcement to myself and the world.

"Fuck it! *I'm moving to California. I am sick to death of shoveling snow in winter and dying of heat in summer.*"

Richard didn't want us to live together and I didn't want another go-nowhere relationship. We had met at a whole health expo, hit it off, and immediately started just being together. But after eighteen months of dating, shuttling between Amherst and Storrs, Connecticut, and now this trip to Nepal, I was ready to go. Michael could come with me or stay in Amherst with his stepmother. Thomas already lived in Boston, and my getting back to Amherst was no big deal if need be.

"*I'm selling the house, getting rid of my stuff, buying a red truck, and driving to the sunshine,*" I told Michael when I returned home. "*I will figure it out as I go along. You can come with me or stay here.*"

A month later I was living in Rancho Santa Fe, California. My parents decided I was crazy, my friends didn't believe I would go, Thomas thought it was great and encouraged me, Michael was angry, and Richard didn't ask me to stay. I cried on the drive all the way across country, didn't know a single person when I got there, and had no idea what might be in store.

I was madly in love with Richard but wanted a rock-solid partner making a path toward cohabitation or marriage. He made it clear that there was no chance. So off I went determined to once again, start my life over. Richard flew over to see me every other month while discovering that my absence was affecting him in a manner he did not expect. After several trips he decided to sell his business and make a life with me.

It wasn't easy for either of us. Richard is a creative, mild-mannered Buddhist, immensely intelligent, somewhat detached, always forgiving, optimistic, generous, and strong. He can fix everything I break, and is a cheerleader for all my desires, except the one I wanted most: marriage.

I was the little French woman on a roller coaster, sometimes pesty, emotional, taking things personally, initiating fun things to do, often reactive, creative, helpful, a basket case during menopause, full of heart, and Richard's muse. California was the place where I could work on my issues, expand my gifts, and start my sound healing business.

We worked it out after he joined me and discovered the ebb and flow of long-term living together. We created a manifesto that reflected our relationship needs and requirements, committing to supporting one another through joy, not judge one another's idiosyncrasies and agreed to revisit it on a regular basis. We invested in couples therapy that helped Richard learn to empathize with my emotions rather than try and fix them. He began to feel comfortable in relationship tho still did not want to marry. I learned how to be more compassionate, patient, and easygoing.

I gave up my attachment to the need to marry. We enjoyed our life together, had wonderful adventures traveling the world, and were happy. I felt secure in the relationship and realized that marriage was just a symbol for the security that was already present. I focused on the many small kindnesses we were able to demonstrate to each other. Whatever I had thought my life was about resurfaced as a realization that being kind to others is the only thing that makes sense, and that being kind to myself is always the first step.

. . .

Several years later, tears spilled down my cheeks as Richard and I took the *bodhisattva* vows at an event with the Dalai Lama, committing ourselves to a compassionate life. Suddenly panicked, I turned to Richard and said, "*Oh, no! This means I'll always have to be nice now. I'm not sure I can do that.*"

I can't, of course. But I keep trying.

Richard

Questions:

- Did you ever experience a hero's journey? Please describe it.
- How did that change your perspective of yourself?
- What qualities did you integrate as a result of that shift?

30

Sound Shaman Road Trip (Who Says Concert Touring Is Romantic?)

One: California

The sun casts its first golden rays over the top of the 9,000-foot-high mountain range in the Sierra Nevadas along highway 395. Miles of high desert plains are peppered with sage-green scrub, short pines, and blotches of low yellow flowers. The still empty road stretches into infinity and my little silver PT Cruiser pushes forward, neck and neck with the colorful boxcars of the very long train peeking in and out between the hills. When we land, PT and I, it's at Sierraville Hot Springs—the halfway point of my tour. Sierraville is a devil-may-care kind of spot that attracts new agers, hippies, and former rednecks who have discovered consciousness and practice Wicca but still drink and smoke (though not here) . . . because, oh well, everyone is human. It is a funky place with a lot of soul. Mineral baths are scattered over 900 acres of wooded property surrounded by grazing cattle, honey-colored wheat fields, and pine-covered mountains. I am gifted a tiny royal blue room with hand-painted silver stars on the ceiling and a comfortable bed—all very '70s—in exchange for doing a short sound healing program for guests here.

The drive to the hot springs from Encinitas marks my change in direction back toward home. When I get there the computer problems that drove me to the brink of my patience—no, truthfully, way past the brink into the out-of-control zone—will still be there. My outgoing email still won't go, my Internet provider will still be totally unhelpful, and my web tech guy will still not know how to fix the problem. But I will be in a much, much better frame of mind to deal with it all because of a shift in perspective. Isn't that what I teach, what all these concerts are about, helping shift a person's perspective from being a victim of life to witness of it?

The teacher is not oblivious to the process. I go through it along with everyone else. Life keeps on offering challenges, each one to practice characteristics that need strengthening within us, ferreting out the gift within the wound. Sometimes it just takes a while to see the gift as we wade though the swamp. And being able to be in the swamp, knowing there is a gift and not being upset about the lurking snakes—now *that's* enlightenment!

Arriving at the hot springs, I am greeted by the sight of a decrepit, rusty VW van. It is beige and the mud-splotched windows reveal pillows, piles of bunched-up clothing, a mattress, some papers, canned goods, and a few cooking implements. It's a total train wreck in there. A small opening in the back where the engine lives is, at the moment, home to what appears to be a white storm. That is, the wispy white-haired head and long straggly beard of a human.

"*This is a classic,*" I say as I stroll by.

The head retreats from the engine.

"*You mean an old hippie and an old van?*"

"*You got it. You are the poster child for something from another time period.*"

White Storm looks right into my soul:

"*I'm trying to fix 'er up to drive to Vermont. My teacher lives there, but she don't want to see me.*" His ice-blue eyes look wild, like they've seen a few too many acid trips. I have no idea what kind of teacher he has but can imagine why she doesn't want to see him.

"*Well, this thing looks like you won't make it out of the driveway to the main road,*" I offer, testing to see if he has a sense of humor. He does.

"*Well, the hurricane there swept away the roads and all her stuff, so I at least want to try to get there to help.*"

Suddenly I'm embarrassed. This wild old guy with a good heart is trying his best to fix his train wreck to help another human being in worse shape than himself. And here I am forming some kind of opinion about him . . . I wish him luck and move along.

I come upon a skinny guy dressed in black with waist-length oily hair copping a smoke on a bench in the shade. He wears copious metal studs and has one very long fingernail, on a pinky finger. His posture is dejected, and he seems achingly depressed, reeking of self-hatred. A group of young women sits in a circle on the grass in front of the lodge, herbal school students from San Francisco who are making a healing salve from berries they picked on the property. They had carpooled there with Depressed Man, and if he decides to go home now they'll be stuck without a ride back, so they're determined to keep him there for the weekend even though he looks like he might kill himself. They really need that ride home.

I head down the path toward the meditation pool, strip down to bare essentials, and bask in the silence of the small, sandy-bottomed pit of hot mineral water surrounded by rocks. There I position myself in warm water up to my neck, lean against the rocks, and let the world disappear. The only sounds are the occasional splash of water, the buzzing bees, and the breeze through the trees. When my skin is wrinkled enough to jolt me out of my reverie, it's time to head back to the lodge.

My mini-workshop takes place in the newly renovated green room. A sweet space that has cubbies for yoga mats, a large wood stove, and new carpeting. Alas—they have installed florescent lights without dimmers. Bad choice, but hey, the rest of the room is a heck of a lot better than it was the last time I was here.

People straggle in. The workshop is free for hot springs guests, who may offer donations. I expect nothing and forget to put out a container to hold these possible gifts.

A twenty-ish herbal school student sweeps into the room with a flourish that says, "*See me.*" Long black wavy hair, curves, and just shy of plump, with an air of false confidence. She speaks with an accent.

"*Where eez your money bowl? I wont to geeve you a nice donation.*"

She says it loudly enough for all to hear. There's something about her that I don't trust. I find that when someone makes a big deal about a donation, the check usually bounces.

But I smile, procure a donation bowl, and thank her for the reminder. She smiles back and announces her gift once again as she places a check in the bowl.

All in all about a dozen people show up and position themselves in a circle around me, like the petals of a lotus flower. It is all very lovely. I chat a bit about how the sounds can help bring them into the present moment to deal with life's conditions. Then I introduce them to the various instruments I have brought and invite them to lie down and enjoy the rejuvenating tonal bath. Since I can't dim the lights, I suggest they cover their eyes with something.

Most of them have a scarf, sweater, or jacket to throw over their eyes. Donation Girl doesn't, so in keeping with my talk about dealing with the realities of life, she simply removes her dress, positions it over her eyes, and sprawls comfortably on the floor, completely naked as she wears no undergarments. About this time, White Storm enters the room looking puzzled and sits in lotus position next to Naked Girl. When the concert is over, she puts her dress back on and helps herself to two of my CDs that are for sale. She lets everyone know she's leaving another check and thanks me profusely for the amazing experience. Later I notice that the total amount of her two donations doesn't even cover the cost of one CD. All I can do is laugh.

After everyone else departs, White Storm comes to sit cross-legged directly in front of me, his untamed beard an unruly cloud. He looks intently at my face as though he is searching for blackheads. Since he doesn't say anything, I just smile and ask, *"So how was that for you?"*

"That was cool. I'm deaf so I missed most of it, but I could tell it was cool."

"You didn't hear anything?"

"Well, some tinkling now and then, and I felt the vibrations. But I mostly didn't hear much of anything. But it was cool. Thank you."

He puts his hand in the donation bowl and pretends to leave a bill. What he leaves is air. The quick gesture reminds me of the times I only had a dollar to put in the church basket when everyone else was leaving $5 and $10 bills. I would fold my dollar up so the people next to me couldn't tell how many bills were in the bundle. I didn't want them to think I was taking advantage, especially when I stayed after the service for the baked goods and coffee. But I wanted to be part of it all and I wanted the cakes, coffee, and fraternity even though I couldn't pay for them. He wanted to be a part of something too. He wanted to give me something, I know, but he had nothing.

I love the gesture, the humanity of this place and people with hearts like White Storm.

Two: Seattle

It is day seven of a nine-day concert tour starting in San Diego, and I have driven fifteen hundred miles to get here. All in all the turnouts have been poor. Tonight's concert starts at seven so the whole day is open for me to explore the city with my new folding Bike Friday, which I've purchased to help pass the sometimes hours between when I arrive somewhere and when I have to set up. But here I sit, angry, disappointed, and emotionally bruised. Only six people have preregistered, but the manager at this spacious and beautiful studio assures me that more will come.

"*For six preregistrations, well, surely at least ten will show up*," she says enthusiastically.

I remind her that my minimum is twenty-five, as is clearly stated in my marketing materials.

Silence, then, "*Oh*." The poor girl does not know what to say.

Shit, another bummer of a turnout and I will have had to hang around the entire day for it. This sucks. As I think this, I adjust my face so the girl doesn't feel too bad. It's not her fault; she's just working the door. The sponsor should have done more to publicize the event. A lot more.

The concert will barely cover expenses. How can sponsors agree to bring people in and then do such a poor job of filling the room? Maybe it's some kind of sign. The entire tour has been like this. Well, it's summer, I am told. *The two gay men with the bookstore in the little town of Garnerville managed to get forty prepaid folks to show up because they cared enough and did whatever they needed to fill the house. So what about Seattle and the other larger towns? Why can't they? I* sense a familiar sting of victimization. Its seduction is strong, as if everything around me is being sucked in to bolster my feelings of despair. People think concert touring is so romantic. Well, it is not.

I enter a Starbucks and order a large drink so I can sit here and work at my computer, only to find out that *this* particular Starbucks doesn't have an Internet connection. See what I mean? Everything is against me. And so the day will unfold with a sinking attitude. *Tick.* I call Richard, hoping to vent and get some sympathy, but he just says, *"Everything will turn out okay, you'll see."* Not what I want to hear. I feel like hanging up on him. *Tock.*

Will I continue to indulge in self-pity or will I choose a different path? Feeling miserable is comfortable and familiar, in a screwed-up kind of way. But an illuminated perspective doesn't come easily, and I know I will have to work to find the better way—the *only* way because otherwise things will certainly get worse, not better.

So here I sit in my mini–snake pit groping for the light. *Jesus, I could be in Pakistan right now, hanging on for dear life with half of my family drowned in the flood or in Haiti starving in the rubbles of the earthquake or in Afghanistan under a hot burka, the unhappy wife of a harsh Taliban husband.*

There is no end to the misery that could befall me and here I am feeling sorry for myself because of poor turnout on this tour? What a prima donna, sitting crestfallen at the Starbucks. On the other hand, it's no good to deny emotions. The trick is to transmute and move forward. After all, anything could happen. The day could unfold in a marvelous way that seems a total tangent from its initial purpose but is not. That is the deep mystery. I sit with this for a moment, see what is happening in my body. Even if I do not buy into this more optimistic perspective, I do know one thing: if I hold a wretched attitude nothing good will come of it and I will alienate any possible gift the day might hold.

The sun begins to peek through the gray Seattle sky. The wind has died down and I suddenly remember that cool bike path I'd noticed the last time I was here, running through what looked like a lovely park. Looking through the window over my left shoulder I can see the river and a few houseboats. That looks worth exploring too.

A woman at a table nearby mentions that there is a free community folk concert down the street. As my spirit opens to the world, the world unfolds its many gifts around me. It has taken all of thirty minutes to arrive at an opening.

Consciousness is simple but not always easy. Transmuting negative into positive can be hard work, and sometimes the reward is not immediately apparent. Sometimes the only reward is that you stop feeling bad. But that is reward enough for me.

Concert Tour

31

BIKING

I can't do this frigging bulldog of a hill. I'm going to walk.

No way! Just keep going—don't look so far ahead—keep your eyes in front of the wheel. Focus on your breath. Focus on your breath.

No! Shit. I've had enough. I am exhausted.

Look, you organized this, now do it. Keep going.

This was the internal conversation that invariably pushed me along in moments of self-perceived trauma. And I mostly always kept going.

My big love affair with movement through nature is biking. Over the past few years it's been the only thing

I want to do to celebrate my birthdays. At sixty-seven I wonder how long it will be possible to continue these week-long bike journeys, going from one new location to the other at the perfect pace: not as slow as walking but not as fast as something with a motor. This is the way to discover the external world while attending to my internal one. Negotiating heat, rain, excruciatingly long uphill climbs, terrifying steep descents with traffic whizzing by. Sucking in glorious landscapes, the scent of wooded or mountain air. Getting to a destination parched, sore, pushed to the limit, exhausted, famished—and delighted to be at the end of another thrilling day spent surviving it all. And the next day and the next, doing it all over again.

People seem to be in awe of those who travel this way, as if they could never do it. But what is the "it" that they could never do? Push past self-perceived limitations? There are so many ways to do that—meditate, run, paint, sing—but I've biked through Ireland, Prince Edward Island, British Columbia, Northern California, Canada, New England. Why? It gifts a sense of liberation. Breezes caress my cheeks and dance in my hair. Breath is steady, rhythm constant. My brain relaxes into the present moment. For miles and miles, sometimes for an entire day, only the sights and sounds of the present moment. No technology, no iPhones, no laundry to do or meetings to get to. Just now. Lungs filling and emptying. There is nothing, not one thing, better than this.

But perfection doesn't come without some trials and tribulations. Big mother hills, for example. Or all-day rain with a head-on wind. A heat wave, an empty water bottle, and fifteen more miles to go. Big trucks splashing dirty water on me as I force myself to keep climbing this relentless hill.

And when I finally arrived at the day's destination and collapse upon the bed, wet and completely worn out, I savor every breath, every muscle, every moment that got me here. The exaltation of having pushed through whatever duress presented itself. The simple joy of a hot shower, a good meal, and a deliciously comfy bed. I look at tomorrow's weather forecast, elated at the prospect of a restful, sunny, hill-less day pedaling through small villages, fertile fields. The perils of today elevate the perfection of tomorrow's promise.

This return to the natural simplicity of each day's biking is a retreat from the chaos of everyday life. And yet within the simplicity, growth comes from staying my course though every situation that presents itself. From finding a way to say yes to everything so that forward movement continues. The emotional muscle strengthens as the physical muscles do. A fundamental principal of good theatrical improvisation is to say *yes* to everything to keep the scene going—otherwise it stops.

The huge fallen tree is blocking my path. I give up. The map is wrong and I now have to backtrack for two hours—I give up. This headwind is so strong I can hardly pedal. I give up. The victim mentality of *I give up* does nothing to advance my transit to the next stopping place. I have to find a way to keep going. And doing that on the bike path strengthens my ability to transfer this skill to all the other areas of my life.

Does this mean I muscle through every situation? No. On a recent trip to Canada, biking in Prince Edward County where the guidebook photos looked wonderful, it soon became clear that the map is not always the territory. There were no dedicated bike paths, only narrow, ill-maintained shoulders with cars and trucks whizzing by. Our prepaid accommodations were terrible. We managed to find a few sweet places to bike but decided to relocate to where we knew there would be better paths. This trip made it clear that a checklist of better questions about biking terrain is essential to future trips. And isn't it the same to navigate the terrain of everyday living artfully, whimsically?

Rummaging around inside myself, I find a knot—solid, like heavy, dense rubber—and a tightness. Like a sort of suspended withholding from my jaw all the way down my body. A deep breath releases the tension momentarily but it returns just as quickly, so it feels like there is no permanent fix—only moment-to-moment consciousness and breath.

All the annoying things that exist—the sound of a clock ticking that prevents sleep, chattering people in the library who ruin concentration, harsh words exchanged with a loved one, politics that cause one's blood to boil, poor food choices while traveling, people who cut in line at the movies—such is the never-ending list of aggravations. Each is reflected perfectly within myself as I hold them all like cherished gifts.

Who is accepting these gifts and why? What purpose do they serve? When one knows something is useless and counterproductive yet still engages with it, what is the benefit? If I am offered a gift that I do not want and so do not accept it, who then owns the gift?

It is within my power to refuse those that are not life sustaining or empowering. To simply not even accept them: the discourteous words directed my way, the degrading look of another, chaos in whatever form. I can see it, observe it, and be a witness without accepting it within myself. I can even make decisions about how to respond to it without allowing it to derail me from my essence.

Is this simple? Yes. Easy? Heck, no. Chaos is seductive and reacting to it provides the ego with a momentary—albeit false—sense of power. To walk through my life negotiating so many levels requires a deep commitment to peace: my own and that of others. So it takes a great deal of practice, often a lifetime's worth, to integrate the lessons needed to live an effective life. Biking compels and guides me in this, teaching me again and again to challenge my self-perceived limits.

Biking

32

THE GIFT IN THE WOUND

First there is the waiting area, gray and sparse. The metal chairs bolted to the floor. The attendant in the cubical behind the glass window who takes my license in exchange for a visitor's pass. Then the series of thick, heavy metal doors. Click. Step through. Click. Step through. A long corridor, the staircase down, ever down.

Past the offices and more glass windows. Then past the angry eyes of men looking out from holding cells. Walking to the elevator with the guard. More metal doors. Clank. Clank. Down again into the abyss.

Another corridor, past more men in single cells. Me, avoiding their eyes, affecting an attitude: *This is no big deal. Just another day.*

Finally we arrive at the large, cafeteria-style open space below the clusters of cells that each hold thirty-two men. Fluorescent lights glare. A television blasts. The men participating today are finishing their boxed lunches. It is 10:30 a.m. and they have been up since 4. Some are sprawled on chairs, legs out, ankles crossed. Some are reading. Many have a vacant look about them. Big men. Small men. Young and old, all shapes and colors. Some scan me wearily and others nod a greeting, flash a smile.

"*Listen up,*" says the warden. "*Time for meditation. Give her your attention.*"

There are some snickers. Some roll their eyes. A few secret hand signals flash between men. Some leave the room, go into their cells, and shut the doors. Somebody flushes. A guard with a million clanking keys comes in and slams the door behind him.

Keep your face neutral. Smile warmly and make eye contact, says my inner voice.

"*It's nice to see you,*" I begin. "*... well, not exactly nice, I wish you weren't here, but you know what I mean.*

"*'Pain is the breaking of the shell that encloses your understanding.' That is a quote from the mystic Khalil Gibran. It has been a support for me all my life. These sessions are meant to invite introspection and deeper exploration into your selves. I will always offer some words of inspiration, and encourage you to find the gift within each challenge. This has been the cornerstone of my own life—finding the gift within the wound. In a sense, we are all both the prisoners and the wardens of our own lives: of our belief systems, of expectations, of conditioning,*

*perspectives. It is only when we allow ourselves to go quiet that
we can let the prison and the warden dissolve and reconnect
with the divine essence of who we are.*

*"This may be new for some of you, but give it a try. Sit back,
relax, and allow yourselves to receive this gift."*

The bowls come out of their rolling box and are set up on
a table that a few of the inmates have brought into the room.

*"Close your eyes and take a few deep breaths. Exhale through
your mouth and just tune in to the sound."*

Slowly, gently, the sound comes up. Those who wouldn't
close their eyes at first—*no fucking way*, they're thinking—
change their minds because what the hell, no harm done.
More bowls, harmonics, more sweet drone of the bowls
singing.

Soon the room gets very quiet. Some heads bob; there
is some snoring. Some men are folded over their knees.
Many sit with backs straight, breath steady and focused.
Faces have relaxed, eyes remain closed.

After twenty minutes, I let the sounds ebb into silence.
"Please take a deep breath, stretch, and slowly open your eyes."
There is a bit of fumbling. A few groans and sighs. It's
quiet in the room and the men look different—they look
better. Some are rubbing their faces and saying, *"Oh, man,
that was awesome."*

For a few moments of their day, the cement quad has
disappeared, the uncomfortable plastic chairs have softened.
The unrelenting voices in their heads have vanished for a
time. There has been some blessed respite.

"Please keep coming back," I hear them say, softly now.

It is an honor to do this work for them as I witness the transformation. All of these men are military vets. Almost all have PTSD. I will be back.

EPILOGUE

Never in a million years did I foresee that I would be working with Tibetan bowls as a sound therapist. As a youngster I saw myself as an actress and a dancer. Every school play was my stomping ground, from Pippi Longstocking in elementary school to summer stock in college, and then I acted professionally. As I look back over my personal roller coaster of challenges on my journey to now, there is not one that I regret. Every difficult situation, heartbreak, and setback taught me resilience. Each scenario offered the choice of whether to sink into victimhood or not. And because we live in a compassionate universe, the lessons I needed to learn were offered over and over again, like a cosmic two-by-four, until I learned them.

There is a lot of payoff in being a victim. It may be uncomfortable, but there is a certain security in staying stuck in a familiar rut instead of dealing with the unknown. Victimhood doesn't always mean falling prey to someone else's expectations either. For me, it was not being able to move past my own limitations, tolerating things in my life that I absolutely had the power to change but did not, or attaching to a negative outlook. Shifting out of the victim mindset takes consciousness and courage. Some people can do it in a moment. I needed a bit longer . . .

It took years for me to see how my relationships with men were impacted by a traumatic childhood event. I kept scanning the universe for things that supported my weakest links and then chose men who would recreate the same pain as the original trauma: abuse and abandonment. It was easy to focus on the scars. But there are many moments of light and love in every single situation, and they are just as present as the harsh moments—when I open to them instead of taking them for granted.

Although fear has been a constant companion throughout much of my life, I have wrestled with it enough to discover this one thing: fear is always around. It keeps coming back. Blazing your path when fear is your companion has a name. It is called *courage*.

For much of my life, fear felt like death. It was an old story of my ego wanting to keep me under its rule. Everyone has their own relationship with fear and feels it in their own unique manner. It is quite seductive, tricking us into believing it is real, but it only takes a shift in perspective to dissolve it in an instant. And this shift in perspective is a conscious choice, so it is important to know what we wish to feel in any given situation. Then we can reason with ourselves and move into something that works better for us. This is really true about almost any emotion, but fear, especially, is like a shape-shifter; it can easily make itself seem real. The strong attraction to staying in fear is that it lets us know we are alive. I now know that the will to live is tantamount to every challenge that befalls us, and it will lead us to greater things if we allow it.

I allowed. I decided to challenge the belief that the universe was unsafe, and doing so rendered trying to control it obsolete. After repeating the same fruitless patterns again and again, the need to shift became painfully obvious to me. I could hold on to my life the way it was and feel stuck, or experience the universe as safe. I finally understood that feeling unsafe is a momentary state of mind whose purpose is to hold me back. This understanding came in waves over time.

On my son Thomas's twenty-first birthday, we jumped out of a plane together. "*Honey, can't you find somebody your own age to do this with?*" But he wanted us to face our fears together as cosmic warriors because I had taught him to deal with fear. Nevertheless, I was frightened, but how could I refuse? Flying through the air from 12,000 feet was incredible, thrilling. The last thing I said to him before we jumped was, "*Whatever you don't want in your life anymore, leave it up here.*" I didn't fully realize then that this was the start of a major metamorphosis for me.

Standing atop a 17,000-foot mountain peak in the Himalayas in 2000 was a pilgrimage to gain perspective about my life. The money for the trip had miraculously been gifted to me at Christmas, and I put it in a CD so I wouldn't spend it on bills. The result of a year and a half of relentless marketing for my polarity therapy business brought me some great clients but only enough income to make ends meet, given two kids, no support, and a mortgage. My self-esteem was low and my energy spent, and I didn't know how to make it all work. Way deep down in my soul, I felt neither competent nor worthy of love. It seemed that the harder I tried, the more failure I experienced, even though I was taking all the right steps. I was simply at the end of my rope. What a blessing!

On that mountaintop I declared that I would change my life. I decided not to compromise myself for the sake of security. The words of the Dalai Lama rang in my mind: *"Take into account that great love and great achievement involve great risk."*

My move to California was like my parachuting free fall: no real plan. But each day was a gift filled with small miracles—a gardening job, a new client, sales of some trinkets I'd brought back from Nepal. I wondered if I was crazy and each day concluded, *Why yes, but it's okay. All I'm really doing is letting go of fear.* Such journeys are always a test of faith.

Maybe it was something about being held in the warmth of the California sun that helped me release the belief that I am defined by what I do, that the amount of money I bring in measures my worth. I embraced myself as being competent, capable, lovable, and intelligent regardless of what I was doing. My decision to engage with the idiosyncrasies of life rather than fight them was a reflection of a newfound trust in the universe. Maybe it won't always be here; it continues to be tested. But somehow I feel more relaxed, alive, and prosperous now than ever before. Giving up control means making space so new things can come into, as well as flow out from, my life.

I spent too many years trying to fit in while being judged for being too sensitive, too offensive, too attached, too needy, too independent, too rigid. It was demoralizing living every day feeling that no matter what, I would never be good enough, big enough, understanding enough, mature enough, or whatever other enoughs I was to ever fit in. In the States, I was Frenchy. In France I was the Yankee cousin. I felt "different" in both countries until I realized I was not marginal, that instead I was a bridge between cultures.

I placed a great deal of focus on relationships with men to whom I was not that important, but each time one of them dissolved, my sense of self dissolved with it. A key to my survival has been to keep finding something, however small, to be grateful for. Gratitude is one of those things that help you deal with shit.

Over the years my ability to transmute negative emotions into patience and compassion has grown, though it is an ongoing process. I did not learn this from my parents, but in the end, it was through their being who they were that I learned a better way.

The task of the Tibetan sacred sound instruments is to widen our perspective, to reconnect us to the divine beings we are, and to bring consciousness to our blind spots so we can enjoy a life of well-being within the constraints of daily life. So we can create our own story of the magnificence of our life.

Much of my life prior to working with them was spent amassing the experiences needed to be of service to others. The blessed school of hard knocks molded every aspect of my life as a teacher, helping me delight in witnessing the empowerment of those I work with. The journey with Tibetan instruments guided my own transformation as they do with others.

It has taken me a lifetime to transmute feelings of hurt and anger toward my sister into those of pity and compassion. Really, though, it does not matter if the target of my wrath is my sister, a pedophile, a mass murderer, or anyone else. When people suffer within, they will do anything possible to make themselves feel better regardless of the human cost. But does this mean I have to sit there and accept the unfathomable?

My work is to recognize what is happening without adding to the drama, to stop inappropriate action the best I can, and to recognize that we all contain within ourselves the seed of every known emotion, gesture, and behavior, from the most brilliant to the most repulsive, and that a change in environment could be the catalyst for things to surface within us that we would never imagine existed.

My sister can no longer hurt me. I see her as she is and have stopped wanting her to be another way. Do I love her? No. But I do feel compassion for her. It is sad to see someone suffering so much and unable to find a positive way of coping. Am I okay about how I feel toward her? I do my best and I know it is my best at this time. Compassion for myself is as vital as it is for others.

My journey has been rich, from my beginnings to the work I do today, performing and teaching, helping people reconnect with their authenticity and stretch past their self-perceived limitations. All the lessons of my past are relevant and essential today ... teachers all. It can take a lifetime to learn to love someone, whether another or ourselves.

My clients who have cancer are on a journey of great courage, despair, hopefulness, hopelessness, surprise, grace, deepening, and betrayal. It can be a roller coaster journey into hell or a great adventure into the finding of their true nature. My work has been to help them connect with their true nature and increase their quality of life no matter how long they will remain in their bodies. This is the journey of healing: the discovery, the embracing of the self, unconditionally and without contracts for physical outcomes. There can be no "if I take care of myself then I will be cured." There can only be the vision of self as perfect as it is, with or without disease, with or without a job, with or without a relationship. As people are able to get closer to that experience, miracles begin to happen. I, of course, am on the same journey of being a witness to my life. My work helps me be better myself at the never-ending journey of wellness.

In my many interviews with trauma victims, as well as in my own life, I have discovered that the two prominent factors in having and maintaining a high state of well-being are *allowing* and *gratitude*. When we stop trying to control outcomes and instead allow the reality of a situation to exist, even discomfort and even pain, and focus on gratitude, miracles happen.

One not so small roadblock is that most of us have no idea how to just let go and allow. There is no magic formula that describes this process. It is an individual exploration that involves many trials—and a great shifting of consciousness. This individual exploration, one that can take weeks or years, *is* the healing process. The compassionate universe gives us opportunity upon opportunity to delve into ourselves. Each challenge is the petri dish for exploration and awakening. Each trial and tribulation is the call to "do it—find yourself." All too often we ignore the call and focus on the issue, thus missing the point. No matter; the universe will not stop just because we do—it will up the ante. It will become louder and louder in its call to action. If we don't get it the first time with a gentle nudge, we will see bigger and bigger challenges come into our lives until we are forced to say the metaphorical "uncle." We are stopped by heartbreak, by illness, by our house burning down, or by death itself. Stopped in a way that leaves us no choice but to do the work, do the exploration, find ourselves.

That's the thing about transitions. No matter when you make them or what they are about, they always require you to pass through a corridor of unknowns that test your faith. In my life, I have welcomed the indefinite nature of starting over even though fear was often a constant companion.

There is a Buddhist saying: "*Anything that annoys you is teaching you patience. Anyone who abandons you is teaching you how to stand up on your own two feet. Anything that angers you is teaching you forgiveness and compassion. Anything that has power over you is teaching you how to take your power back. Anything you hate is teaching you unconditional love. Anything you fear is teaching you courage to overcome your fear. Anything you can't control is teaching you how to let go."*

Some people seem to do that pretty quickly. Some never seem to get there. When my father died of cancer, he got angrier as he lost more and more control. In the end he was insulting the doctors, the nurses, the hospice aides—all the people who were trying to help him. How sad to end one's life in such a state. He probably never understood that he had a choice to keep fighting a losing battle and implode with rage—which he did—or he could let go and find peace, which he seemed to do only at the last moment of his life in order to pass on. Like sleep, death is something that requires surrender, something we release into.

My relationship with my mother has always been cantankerous. It has taken decades to respond to her with compassion and humor and to live up to my own desire to be a good daughter despite all the triggers that are set off within me. In my adulthood, I know she did the best she could and was unprepared for the challenges of her adult life.

Life now is abundant with blessings. I see my children go through their paces as they find their way, and I finally have means to help them access their dreams in ways I could not have before. I have grown enough to enjoy an intimate and lasting relationship with my partner, Richard, since 1998. I have produced works that hopefully enhance the lives of others. As I continue to stay upright in an ever-changing universe as if walking on Jell-O, I recognize that life, every bit of it, is indeed a wonderful gift.

It's time to write your own story while looking back at your life with gratitude. Just begin and let the muse take you.

ACKNOWLEDGMENTS

I would like to thank all of the people, living or passed on, who have been part of my life, in a supportive or a non-supportive manner. Each has been a teacher on an amazing journey rich in experience and opportunity. They are the sources of this book. Thank you also to my wonderful partner, Richard Rudis, for being my unconditional cheerleader, and to my dear friend and writing partner Richard Hawk, who worked with me for hours and years as this book took shape. This is the second book Sheridan McCarthy has edited for me. I cannot say enough about her constructive feedback and excellent work. She made the process fun, and working with her has taught me a great deal about writing. Thank you.

ABOUT THE AUTHOR

Diáne Mandle is an internationally known author, recording artist (Sounds True), Tibetan bowl practitioner, and educator, and is the only state certified practitioner-instructor in California. Diáne has given more than two hundred fifty educational concert programs in thirty-two states, as well as in India, Costa Rica, Mexico, and St. Croix. She has been a frequent guest presenter at the Museum of Making Music, California State University San Marcos, the Golden Door, The Chopra Center, Rancho la Puerta, and on KPBS. She is a featured expert in the video series *Tao—Living in Balance*, along with healers such as Dr. Wayne Dyer and John Gray.

Diáne maintains a private sound healing practice in southern California, where she also owns and operates the Tibetan Bowl Sound Healing School. She has been part of the integrative therapy team at the San Diego Cancer Center in Encinitas and has developed a successful sound healing program for incarcerated veterans with PTSD. Her first book, the award-winning *Ancient Sounds for a New Age*, (1998), was also published in France in October 2020.

Diane